THE ENTERPRISE

BLACK BOX THINKING

PART ONE

DESIGNOVATION: THE PROCESS FOR BRINGING PLANS INTO REALITY.

BY D.F.MCKEEVER

AMAZON EDITION

ISBN:9781791861360

COPYRIGHT 2011 D.F.MCKEEVER

DISCLAIMER & PRIVACY POLICY THIS BOOK IS LICENSED FOR YOUR PERSONAL ENJOYMENT ONLY. THIS IS THE SOLE PROPERTY OF DESIGNOVATION. ALL RIGHTS ARE RESERVED. NO PART OF THIS WORK MAY BE REPRODUCED OR TRANSMITTED IN ANY FORM OR BY ANY MEANS; ELECTRONIC OR MECHANICAL, INCLUDING, PHOTOCOPYING, RECORDING OR BY ANY INFORMATION STORAGE OR RETRIEVAL SYSTEM, WITHOUT THE WRITTEN PERMISSION OF THE COPYRIGHT OWNER. DESIGNOVATION SHALL NOT BE HELD LIABLE TO ANY PERSON OR ENTITY WITH RESPECT TO ANY LOSS OR DAMAGE CAUSED OR ALLEGED TO BE CAUSED DIRECTLY OR INDIRECTLY BY THE INFORMATION CONTAINED WITHIN THIS WORK. FURTHERMORE, NO PART OF THIS MAY BE REPRINTED OR RESOLD. THIS EBOOK MAY NOT BE RE-SOLD OR GIVEN AWAY TO OTHER PEOPLE. IF YOU WOULD LIKE TO SHARE THIS BOOK WITH ANOTHER PERSON, PLEASE PURCHASE AN ADDITIONAL COPY FOR EACH RECIPIENT. IF YOU'RE READING THIS BOOK AND DID NOT PURCHASE IT, OR IT WAS NOT PURCHASED FOR YOUR USE ONLY, THEN PLEASE RETURN TO KINDLEBOOKS.COM THANK YOU FOR RESPECTING THE WORK OF THIS AUTHOR.

LEARN MORE:

HTTP://WWW.DESIGNOVATION.CO.UK

https://youtu.be/uwp7A3U_5hs

*This is dedicated to my
husband Ronnie and my three children
thank you for your
unconditional love, support and encouragement.
To my Mum thank you for your
creativity and Dad for your relentless
entrepreneurial spirit.*

Contents

	Page
Introduction	6
Chapter 1 The Black Box 1976	8
Chapter 2 The Worlds Creativity Park 2065	12
Chapter 3 The Black Box introduction	21
Chapter 4 The Tour	26
Chapter 5 I. The leverage of others labour and skills	30
Chapter 6 The Associates	39
Chapter 7 II. The Creation of a definite plan & purpose	45
Chapter 8 The Leader	51
Chapter 9 III. Serving others with specialised knowledge or skills	58
Chapter 10 To Serve	67
Chapter 11 IV. Persistence & the understanding of human desires and fears	72
Chapter 12 The Sales Person	78
Chapter 13 V. Material wealth through the mastery of financial education	85

	Page
Chapter 14 The Book Keeper	99
Chapter 15 VI. The power & orchestration of organised systems, processes & people.	105
Chapter 16 The Analyst	113
The Summary	122
Note	125
Bibliography	131

Introduction

Welcome to Part Two of 'The Designovation ® Philosophy', in Part One I introduced you to the six characteristics which embody every great entrepreneur, the symbol of the Creative Entrepreneur 'The Entrepreneur; White Ball Thinking'. Whether you are someone aspiring for success in your life, career or business you will now understand the qualities, tools & skills necessary as an individual to design and sustain the energy and passion to build a great career or enterprise.

In this book Part Two 'The Enterprise; Black Box Thinking' I will share the lessons I have learnt from my fascination of 'Great Enterprises' and my analysis from studying, listening & observing entrepreneurs since my teens. This book will challenge your thoughts on the role of creativity in business and the 'small business owner' by sharing the advice of fellow entrepreneurs and business owners rather than 'theorist of businesses'.

We will return to the Creativity Park and reveal a very different set of principles, designed for the Entrepreneur. Here we will reveal the structures, supports and foundations to any great business and introduce the six key functions one has to master if you wish to build a sustainable business fit for the 21st Century. This book will share the insights and observations of great entrepreneurs, business strategists, leaders, business philosophers and economists from Sam Walton, W. Edward Deming, Elon Musk, Sir Alex Ferguson to Adam Smith.' The Enterprise; Black Box Thinking & The Entrepreneur; White Ball Thinking' is only the first in a series of books introducing the various elements of the Designovation® principles and how creativity is central to achieving sustained growth, innovation and a new ethical approach to business. Before we begin a quote from one of the Worlds Greatest Manager:

"Before you can field a great team, you have to build a great organisation and all the elements have to be assembled properly." Scotsman, Sir Alex Ferguson.

PART TWO

Chapter 1

The Black Box 1976

The back door of the kitchen opened and my father entered into the dimly lit hallway appearing unfamiliarly despondent and distant as he shook the rain from his coat and then hung it on the coat rack. As he entered the kitchen he spoke quietly under his breath to my mother, faintly mentioning my grand fathers name before my mother reached out to comfort him in a tight embrace.

I sat by the fire place with my head down pretending to be busy sketching with my pencil and notebook. As I sat wondering to myself what was going on, my sisters sat in the other room watching television and chattering away like any other normal Sunday evening.

Subdued and preoccupied both my parents went about their usual Sunday night routine, my mother stood ironing our school clothes as my father rallied us around to polish our school shoes for the next day. As we stood in the kitchen a faint knock could be heard from the back door and my father looked at the kitchen clock apprehensively.

"Who is chapping our door at this time of night Duncan?" said my mother curiously.

My father slowly made his way to the back door and momentarily reappeared in the darkened hallway with the silhouette of a tall broad man stooped and standing in front of him in silence. As my father directed him into the kitchen and to a chair at the dinner table, we all scurried away into the living room realising that the man was a stranger. As I peeked my head around the corner of the kitchen door the man sat in silence with his long unkempt silver hair and beard and old dirty, tattered clothes. As I looked under the table his leather shoes were cracked, worn and torn and held together with two pieces of string tied together as laces.

I was bemused as my mother & father behaved as if this was a regular Sunday night occurrence, nothing quite out of the ordinary. My mother immediately heat up some left over soup and placed the bowl with a plate of bread on the table in front of him. The man hurriedly lifted the spoon with his eyes and head still stooped over the table. Even though his appearance was of a tramp his build, stature and presence conveyed something very different. His hands were long and slim and his worn knitted gloves revealed the fingers and hands not of a working man but gentry.

A few minutes later my father reappeared in the room with an old long coat, jumper, scarf, gloves and an old pair of his pit boots & black snit socks. As my mother cleared and washed away the empty plates she made up a food bag while the man emptied the contents of his old worn coat and placed them on the table. Among the loose change, was a box of matches, a pen knife and a leather pouch.

As the man dressed himself in the clothes and boots my father had given him, he raised his head and with his piercing steel blue eyes looked across the room at me, before removing a black piece of wood shaped like a cube from the leather pouch placing it in the centre of the table. Before I knew it my mother handed him the food bag, he picked up the loose change, box of matches and pen knife and placed them in his coat pocket.

He then took a deep breath and gave a gentle sigh of relief, as he cast me a second look with a contented smile.

Without a single word and nothing but a simple nod to my mother and father the man stood tall and upright as he made his way out of the kitchen and into the dimly lit hall vanishing into the dark night like a soul with a lightened load. The evening's strange events past, and within minutes everything resumed to normal as my sisters and I went about our nightly chores before finally going to bed.

Early the next morning my father sat us all down, and gently broke to us the difficult and heart breaking news that one of my earliest child heroes my papa had passed away during the night.

Chapter 2

The Worlds Creativity Park 2065

Annie entered the South Gate entrance that led directly to the South Garden, clutching an old brown leather bound book and a small leather pouch. She passed through the grand gates where the face recognition cameras instantly approved her identity and access to enter the park, as her audio fashioned hear-ring chip synchronised with the parks communications system.

It was a beautiful summers evening, the trees were in full bloom and amidst the beautiful calming silence she could hear the gentle twittering of the birds perched in the trees. Once again Gran's advice was right, instantly Annie felt less confused, at ease and relaxed.

She made her way along the winding shingle path that Gran had suggested to an empty clearing where the largest oak tree in the park stood and sat down with her back resting on its trunk securing the best viewing point of the large Musk Dome. As she waited for the exclusive private tour of the Creativity Park to begin, a group of pre-selected guests entered the South Garden many from their appearance appeared to be young students, graduates and business people. As dusk approached everyone waited patiently for the Hologram show to begin.

Annie had completed her College studies in Acting and Drama and after spending her weekends and summers applying what she had learnt in various stand-up & comedy clubs she knew once and for all that she wanted to build her own business.

After the trials and tribulations of listening to business advisors, consultants and academics with the same parrot fashion narrative, she realised that something didn't ring true, they were all theorists. The majority of them had very unambitious ideas with a limited vision of what was possible. The majority of them had never owned or built their own business, never mind being brought up in a family in business with any experience of building something from their *own* toile and hard earned cash.

The single question Annie kept asking herself was:
"If they knew so much about business why were they not out building, creating and operating their own business or enterprise?"

As the sky darkened the faint sound of a single piper announced the start of the show. The two largest solar-mast windmills in the park with their fine high-tech blades and colour changing technical textile masts opened and elevated to face the dome, each placed strategically in the south location of the Park. And like giant projectors beamed the projection of a film across one side of the Musk Dome. The lights of the dome dimmed making it almost invisible and the south garden turned into a 1960's drive in movie screen minus the cars. As the sound of the single piper faded my audio fashioned hear-ring chip began commentating on the movie projection.

We were taken back in time to 2018 when the landscape was of multi-storey buildings, wind turbines and remnants of the Industrial revolution; steel works, ship building and heavy manufacturing. The movie moved into hyper speed as the area we now sat on was flattened, excavated and redesigned to build the foundations of the Worlds Creativity Park.

We watched as industrial plant equipment and drilling rigs carved out the surrounding terrain, filling bore holes in strategic spots to support the giant architectural structure of the Worlds Creativity Centre. We watched as a vast upright oval cavern was gradually assembled from concrete panels deep beneath the earth. Mid way through its construction an internal walkway was added circling the circumference of the cavern with 6 doorways leading off to tunnels and chambers buried deep in the earth under the gardens of the Creativity Park. We watched as the vast white ball was winched into place and simultaneously its protective square box frame was assembled with 6 separate supporting panels, 2 of them reinforced to stabilise the foundations and surface of the ball. The black box & white ball were suspended underground in the vast concrete cavern encasing with the white ball that would transform level one into the underground Inverted Atrium and level two and three into the Designovator's room and protruding Musk Dome.

We watched the two year development of the site from an industrial wasteland to its beautiful expansive gardens & loch bringing together

The Inspirational Garden, The Library, The Dream Room, The Designovation Studio, The Great Pioneers Hall and The Time Machine. They commentated on the various individuals that had came together as a team with one shared common goal contributing their unique individual expertise and skills in engineering, architecture, design, innovation, electronics, environmentalism. Discussing how relationships and friendships with great leaders of Industry visionaries in the renewable energy sector, computing, manufacturing, civil engineering, communications, science and technology became the catalyst to complete the vision for the park.

As the hologram show ended a secret doorway appeared at the South garden below the Musk Dome as each guest was invited to take the exclusive private tour at their own leisure. Gradually some of the guests made their way to the secret doorway while others sat enjoying the peacefulness of the Park.

Annie sat resting against the large oak tree and took a few private moments to reflect. She sat reflecting on the enterprising stories and lessons she had been told over the years from her Grand mother about Mary & Duncan. How Duncan Seniors first business was as a fruit man selling fruit & vegetables door to door with his horse & cart, followed by his various enterprising adventures with Mary.

Her greatest inspiration came from the letters her Gran read to her about Mary's commendations applauding her entrepreneurial spirit, sales, management & organisational skills while simultaneously prioritised her uncompromising responsibilities & role as a mother of eight. Annie loved Mary's commitment to her role as a mother something that was never overshadowed or compromised in her pursuit of a career.

All letters she now kept neatly folded in her leather bound book;

JOHN ENGLAND

MESNES PARK, WIGAN
LANCASHIRE

Tuesday, 14th June, 1966

TO ALL AREA MANAGERS, ASSISTANT MANAGERS AND SUPERVISORS.

Ladies and Gentlemen,

      We are enjoying another wonderful season, and it might interest you to know that we are far ahead of any of our associated Companies in terms of production. That's the way I like it, of course, and with the Conference coming up in July, it's nice to know that we can walk in there with a fine degree of confidence and maybe just the trace of swagger in our step.

      One of our ladies, MRS. BURNS of SCOTLAND who, unfortunately, for domestic reasons, cannot attend the Conference, would be crowned the Queen of them all if she was there, because last week, she broke a two year old record and produced 74 starters from 9 girls, and one of those nine girls, only produced one starter which meant that eight of them produced 73, and that, my friends, is "some going", or is it, "going some"?

      The previous record, also held in Scotland from a similar number of girls was 72 starters, but 72, bah! kid stuff, the new figure is 74. Any offers?

      Mrs. Burns has always been a top flight Supervisor and has appeared in my news letters many times, so she is no stranger to you, but what you didn't know, is that Mrs. Burns is also the Mother of a large family. I daren't tell you how many because you wouldn't believe me, but I can tell you that everyone of her children are a credit to her and her husband and to each other. They all help with the cooking, the cleaning, the shopping, the making and the mending, which, when you come to think of it, is the right way to bring up kids, and having got that side of her life organised properly, it's mere routine to get her staff organised properly, and those 74 starters rather suggest that she is winning.

      Incidentally, those 74 starters have rushed Mrs. Burns up to join the exclusive ranks of the Supervisors with 400 or more starters, and at week 18, anybody with 400 or more, really is exclusive. The list so far consists of:

      MRS. VEGLIO 448, MRS. CARTER 436, MRS. EDGELL 435, MRS. LOFTHOUSE 435, MRS. BURNS 430, MRS. CAREY 425 and MRS. LEVY 400.

      Here now, are a couple of news items concerning staff

/cont

Footnotes: Great Universal Stores was founded in 1900. During the 1930s a second catalogue named "John England" was also produced. In 1937 GUS acquired Kays Catalogue. Kays stayed as a separate company until the 1980s. In 2004, the company sold its traditional catalogues division to the Barclay twins who merged into their Littlewoods Empire.

JOHN ENGLAND

SBO/SR

MESNES PARK, WIGAN
LANCASHIRE

29th March, 1965

Mrs. M. Burns,

Dear Mrs. Burns,

    We are well blessed who are twice blessed, but 30 times blessed is forcing the pace to a point when it ought to pay off in hard cash, and of course, that is what this letter is all about, a jovial little scribble to tell you that 30/-d is literally on its way to you.

    I hope that you are treating all this money that you are earning, with some respect, and that you have got a fair amount hidden away under the floor boards in the front bedroom, because one day, with this flair you have for acquiring the right staff, you might want to start a Mail Order Company of your own.

    They tell me that it needs £5,000,000 to start on the scale that we are accustomed to, so please save your pennies, and when you have got enough,, I am coming to work for you.

    You're a good girl Mrs. Burns, and it is a pleasure to write to you this way, but I hope that you will recognise, that between the lines of nonsense, I am very proud of the fact that you are on my Sales Force.

    Best wishes, and
      sincerely,

S.B. Oldham
SALES MANAGER

DIRECTORS: R. HARRIS (CHAIRMAN) - S. W. BARKER - J. D. PARRY - S. I. HARRIS, A.C.A. - W. ISHERWOOD - J. J. STRAWBRIDGE

Smiling to herself and taking her grandmothers shrewd advice, Annie began to reread the first few chapters of her book along with the letter she found tucked inside its cover.

Chapter 3

The Black Box Introduction

Dear Entrusted,

I bestow this gift into your safe keeping and hope that it brings you the blessings and joys it has bestowed myself and my loved ones.

Before you begin this journey I ask that in return you simply commit to four basic principles and by doing so gain the full appreciation and benefit from the contents of this book that accompanies the two paper weights:

I Read both manuscripts and the book in its entirety.
II Commit to mastering the six elements of the black box and white ball.
III Open your mind; be inquisitive, creative, questioning and develop your own thinking.
IV Entrust its teachings in the spirit of your children.

The contents of this book will take you on a journey to discover two philosophies. Life and nature sustains itself through a natural balance of opposites. The teachings of the 'black box' and 'white ball' are two separate and very opposite philosophies which when combined can create genius.

The material power of the Black Box will help you discover your material purpose in life. The black box is a fixed stationary object with limited movement. It is a systems centred thinking focused on simplified order, clear disciplined roles, functions, plans and strategies. It derives its power and success from follower personalities who like order and rules and the need for conformity, conventionality and structure. Each side of the black box cannot function independently without influencing and impacting on each other side of the box. The Black Box has six basic functions:

I. Human Resources; leverage of others labour and skills.
II. Management; the Creation of a definite plan & purpose.
III. Products or Services; serving others with specialised knowledge or skills.
IV. Sales; persistence and the understanding of human desires and fears
V. Finance; material wealth through the mastery of financial education.
VI. Operations; the power and orchestration of organised systems, processes & people.

The creative power of the White Ball will help you discover your spiritual purpose in life. The White ball is a free flowing moving object, bouncing, rolling and always in perpetual motion. Unlike the Black box which is static, rigid & fixed it thrives on freedom and movement like snow flakes in the wind. It is a powerful human centred philosophy. The personality of the white ball is very similar to the spirit of a child the youthful dreamer, the believer & the free thinker. The White Ball has six essential characteristics:

I. The Spirit; Passion

II. The Believer; Faith.

III. The Designer; Vision.

IV. The Inventor; Ideas.

V. The Gambler; Risk.

VI. The Rebel; Courage.

I hope that within this book you will discover the wisdom and insight to fulfil your dreams.

Anonymous x

The Black Box Introduction

Before you study this manuscript one must note that the Black box philosophy is a systems centred thinking rather than human centred thinking, the Black box represent 6 separate but interlinked teachings that have been taught and passed down by teachers and elders from one generation to the next. One must remember that each side is essential to it's over all stability, the absence of a side or function will create vulnerability and instability. The six key principles or functions of the black box are:

I. Human Resources; leverage of others labour and skills.

II. Management; The Creation of a definite plan & purpose.

III. Products or Services; serving others with specialised knowledge or skills.

IV. Sales; persistence and the understanding of human desires and fears.

V. Finance; material wealth through the mastery of financial education.

VI. Operations; the power and orchestration of organised systems, processes & people.

The black box philosophy is like a box, it is a fixed stationary object rigid with limited movement, defined parameters, thinking and rules. Each side cannot function independently without influencing and impacting on each other side of the box and its functions. It creates results through simplified order, clear disciplined roles & plans and strategies. It gains power and strength with its philosophy appealing to follower personalities who like order, rules, conformity and conventional structures.

It is the essential ingredient that has created great historical economic, military and religious forces through out history. When you create a perfect black box each side of the box synchronises together like a unique piece of technical engineering. Before you proceed with the first lesson please take note that the black boxes strength can also be its greatest weakness. Its lack of human centred thinking can make it void of personal initiative and emotional intelligence and be threatened by extinction due to its lack of creativity or innovation.

Chapter 4

The Tour

Annie briskly walked towards the entrance of the secret tunnel which would take her to the underground section of the Creativity Park.

It wasn't long before Annie came to an abrupt halt as she crossed the threshold of the tunnel onto the internal walkway that encircled the concrete cavern. The full expansion of the Parks control centre was revealed in its full magnitude and scale. Before her stood the spectacle of a glass ball the height of a fifteen storey building supported and contained within a large black box frame with six round protruding windows on each side of the box.

The contrast between the backdrop of the giant white concrete panels suspended around the control centre with the bright clear glass ball and the black box frame created a startling clinical airy environment inconceivable underground.

The ball was split into 3 levels; level one the concealed inverted atrium floor and level two the open plan Designovator's Room, level three the external musk dome only visible from the Park. Where Annie stood she could see directly into the giant open plan Designovator's room with the six internal elevators that transported associates & guests between the three levels of the white ball. From the internal walkway she could clearly see six cavern openings positioned evenly around the internal walkway and above each square doorway a different inscription and quote carved deep into the concrete.

As Annie stood on the threshold of the tunnel and internal walkway she watched as two separate plinths emerged slowly from the floor. While through her hear-ring chip she was asked to step forward in front of the plinth representing her private tour. One at a time from left to right the two plinths emerged from the floor with a suspended holographic image appearing above each of them.

The first plinth on her left emerged with the holographic image of a white glass ball illuminated inside with a bright radiant light the ball then elevated from its stationary position and began spinning with great speed to generate an array of luminescent colours. The narrator introduced the 'Designovator's ® Room' explaining that entry to this tour was by private invitation only. She described how this was the heart and creative hub of the Worlds Creativity Park, the essence of what all the associates called the 'White Ball'. This is where you would discover the secrets of how the Park continued to excite, enthuse and motivate its associates and simultaneously evolve, grow and reinvent itself.

The second plinth emerged with the holographic image of a black box. The narrator explained that the 'Black Box' tour would teach you the secrets of how like the Creativity Park anyone can design, engineer, plan and operate a sustainable and competitive revolutionary business or enterprise.

The narrator went on to say:
"Our tour will demonstrate that a business is a business is a business whether you are a small business or large corporation it doesn't matter, they all have the same 6 functions and sides to their business. Through out the centuries this has and never will change. But to create a strong solid business or using our analogy a strong "Black Box" you need 6 sides that integrate, synchronise & work together. A franchise business on one level is a great example of a synchronised business a turn-key operation. That is why Companies like Disney, McDonalds, and KFC worked so well in the early 21st century. Unfortunately in today's climate to be just a strong "black box business" is not enough, to really succeed your business has to be significantly more creative, innovative & smarter than the competition with a culture and way of thinking

which embraces, lives and breathes creativity. And like the Black Box structure in the Creativity Park every great business has at least one or two functions or sides of their business that is significantly more creative than the competition. Finally please remember that every remarkable business, enterprise or entrepreneur started life as a small 'black box' in the palm of your hand with the seed of one person's idea".

As the presentations ended without hesitation Annie stepped forward in front of the second plinth and let the 'Black Box' tour begin.

Chapter 5

I. Human Resources: The leveraging of labour and skills.

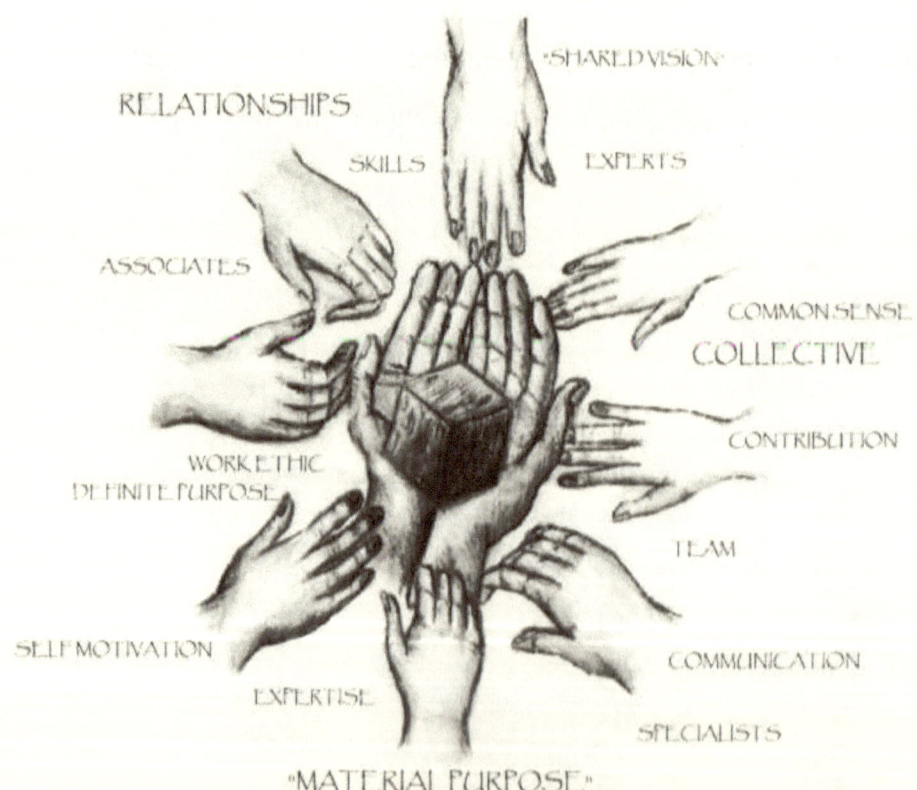

Our success is defined by the combined value and strength of our humanity, the relationships in our communities, family units, society and workforce. The most essential ingredient to all achievement is the will and combined effort of our human resources from the individual to the collective. No individual person or society, culture or enterprise can sustain itself independently.

Fundamentally we must first start with the individual, defining and identifying our true individual role and purpose. We must first understand our part and role in this universe if we wish to ever serve our material purpose in life. It is essential that we find our role and place within society where we can provide for ourselves and our dependants and contribute in benefiting and supporting the collective. Any organisation, enterprise or group who come together in the name of a single cause and collectively understand their individual material purpose in life will be a passionate force to be reckoned with. If you learn any single lesson from this manuscript, it is to teach and share this single lesson to your children.

One must discover and find in life ones single "Material purpose"

Without the understanding and application of this fundamental lesson one will move aimlessly through life without focus, clarity and vision. Many have come to regret the wasted energy of their youth only discovering their purpose of life in old age now without the wealth & health and freedom to achieve its fulfilment. This single teaching has outlived the test of time, it is a lesson which has been taught and passed down from the wise and learned from one generation to the next through times of success, conflict and strife.   Croesus, adviser to Cyrus, King of the Persians once said;

"I am reminded O King, and take this lesson to heart, that there is a wheel on which the affairs of men revolve, and its mechanism is such that it prevents any man from being always fortunate...... This same wheel that prevents any man from being always fortunate may provide also that no one shall be always unfortunate, provided he will take possession of his own mind and direct it to the attainment of some Definite Major Purpose in Life."

A lack of a definite major purpose in life will leave us wandering aimlessly through our social and professional roles in life. With the knowledge of our individual material purpose we can seek out roles and environments where our skills and talents leverage greatest benefit and results in serving the world.

We must also recognise that we will never fulfil the full potential of our material purpose without the combined wisdom of knowing our spiritual self and our 'creative purpose'. As human beings we have both our physical and spiritual selves which cannot fully function with out each other, our physical selves ultimate purpose is to embody, serve and protect the spiritual self which unlike the physical self is everlasting.

Develop a group of "associates" from different disciplines, interests and areas of expertise.

No man or woman is an island and as such everyone needs the benefit of good and valuable relationships to progress in life, socially and professionally. The secret is not necessarily in the number of associates we have but in the quality of character and skill each individual has to offer in fare exchange for your services to achieve both your common goals. All great achievement has come from individuals that have developed a positive magnetism that attracts like minded individuals. Associates with a positive magnetism and with a positive and pleasing personality will always motivate and attract greater benefit to your enterprise than a negative pessimist that can only see problems rather than simply challenges.

Aim to develop a group of associates from different disciplines, interests and expertise whether in your workplace, enterprise or community to strengthen your black box. A lack of council or expertise from a single face of the black box will weaken its stability and effectiveness. Always be willing to welcome associates who positively challenge your perceptions and opinions and that broaden your thinking and ideas. It is often your greatest adversaries that challenge you the most and encourage you to question your decisions and thinking and motivate you to greatest success. I would rather share the company of an associate that will positively question my decisions rather than an associate that will always agree with me.

Promote the Continual Development of Skills

It is essential that you promote the habit of continually developing ones skills and knowledge. Anyone with a definiteness of purpose will have the passion and drive to continually strive to build and renew their resources of information, ideas and expertise in achieving and sustaining their material purpose. Skills and knowledge can come in many forms, from people, street or book smarts to skilled repetition and practice of an area of expertise.

The greatest experts and minds are those that develop the humility to 'listen more than they speak' and seek council from those that take action and produce tangibles rather than the theorists that spend their lives talking and creating nothing. Life is a continual process of learning and developing, when we stop learning and developing we stop living and progressing.

Essential Skills: a work ethic, self motivation and common sense.

Our human resources are the back bone to any black box. It is essential that we are skilful in recognising the principles of a strong reliable community and work force. The ability to see potential and discern beyond image, class and prejudice is an essential skill in defining the human resources face of the black box. It is essential that you learn how to discern when one possess the most simple but most essential of skills i.e. self motivation, a work ethic and basic common sense.

The most unlikely of candidates that demonstrates self motivation and a work ethic will out perform and leverage profits you will never obtain from the most skilled and qualified. The great attribute of the working classes is their work ethic. Once the indelible scars of poverty and hunger are replaced by the taste of reward one has an insatiable motivation for something better and more rewarding. A good work ethic and resourcefulness is rarely shared amongst the wealthy because it is a product of lack and an absence of privilege.

The most overlooked and forgotten skill is simply common sense. Common sense is a skill not everyone can be taught or possess and is often in short abundance. The greatest problems are often created from a lack of common sense but only solved as a result of common sense.

The will to give more than we receive

The most important principle of our Human Resources is our 'Will to give more than we receive'. For a fare and balanced society that takes care of its disadvantaged, elderly and sick we must instil in our children the principle and will to give more than we receive. Every member of society must provide an honest exchange and contribution of labour and effort to receive any form of material or financial reward. Otherwise we will create a society on all class levels of greed, idleness void of integrity and personal pride.

The Art of Communication

One of humanities greatest art forms is the skill of communication. All the greatest academic honours in the land are of no value to man or beast if one cannot fulfil the simple task of sitting across a room and initiating the art of conversation with another human being. The art of conversation is essential in building rapport, relationships and alliances. It is a skill that can bring down barriers, open doors and motivate and persuade others. Without it one cannot buy, sell, trade or negotiate. The skill to communicate and relate to those of a differing, class, culture or means will enhance your efforts in motivating and attracting new associates to achieve your definite purpose. Communication is essential to all success in personal relationships and life.

Summary

I. One must discover and find in life ones single "Material Purpose in Life"

II. Develop a group of "associates" from different disciplines, interests and areas of expertise.

III. Promote the Continual Development of Skills.

IV. Essential Skills: a work ethic, self motivation and common sense.

V. The will to give more than we receive

VI. The Art of communication

Chapter 6

The Associates

"The leverage of others labour & skills."

Annie began making her way round the internal walkway that encircled the concrete cavern passing the 6 square doorways with their black wooden frames. As she passed each doorway she read each separate inscription carved deep into the concrete in large Celtic script.

I "The leverage of others labour and skills."
II "The Creation of a definite plan & purpose."
III "Serving others with specialised knowledge or skills."
IV "Persistence and the understanding of human desires and fears."
V "Material wealth through the mastery of financial education."
IV "The power and orchestration of organised systems, processes & people."

As Annie approached the first doorway the narrator invited her to enter its reception room which looked like a perfectly formed black box with wooden panelled walls, floor & ceiling. As she entered the dimly lit room, the black wooden door closed slowly behind her and a single holographic portrait appeared of the Great Welsh social reformer and one of the founders of the cooperative movement Robert Owen and below it the quote;

"There is but one mode by which man can possess in perpetuity all the happiness which his nature is capable of enjoying- that is by the union and co-operation of all for the benefit of each."

At that dozens of holographic portraits appeared on the walls with portraits of each team member employed at the Park and below their name the single title 'Associate'. Momentarily the holographic portraits faded and disappeared as a second door appeared. The door opened to the human resources sector of the control centre and as Annie entered the brightly lit room she noticed the large hand written words on the furthest facing wall;

"Have the Courage to take a Risk & share your Values, Passion, Faith, Vision and Ideas with the World".

Annie entered the room to the background noise of buzzing activity and an expansive open plan room full of individuals of every age and nationality vocal and animated with enthusiasm. The energy in the room was positive and contagious and as Annie stood surveying the room every individual who passed her acknowledged her with a welcome, hello or friendly remark. The surroundings were warm, friendly and inviting and everyone she observed exhibited a sense of purpose and focus in their brisk walk, upright stature and gestures.

The expansive open plan room had an inviting café in the centre of the room and 5 cinematic screens to the right of the room with live feeds from the other sectors. To the left of the room were four adjoining square conservatory rooms for recruitment, training, team building and design thinking. Every associate wore the same immaculate hi-tech uniform with the same colour, trim, detailing and fastenings but in different styles, shapes & silhouettes to compliment their age, shape & personality. The surroundings exuded order, discipline and focus but with an underlying spirit and atmosphere of freedom, self expression and individualism.

The attention to detail displayed in the design of the Human Resources room showed a definite vision of how the Park valued their employees. From the choice of interior colours, the natural programmed lighting, the uniforms, dress code to the use of technology to interconnect with other departments to create an inclusive single layered culture. Everything from the positioning of the café with its large comfy sofas and friendly staff in the centre of the room was designed to encourage a sense of community.

Annie approached the recruitment room to her left, and from the external viewing window with its one way glass she observed the processes and systems the Park used for recruiting new associates. The instructor explained that they were joining a company culture unlike anything they had experienced before. The instructor explained how its Human Resources model was inspired by the principles of the legendary W. Edwards Deming and companies like W. L. Gore.

Most people think of Deming as the genius statistician who revitalised Japanese industry, yet his understanding that people 'are the business' is what equally contributed to his success. He understood that people flourish in a positive environment when given the freedom to use their brains, the right tools & systems to continuous innovation and improvement not a culture of 'FEAR'. He knew that people fundamentally take pride in what they do and everyone has different talents and abilities to bring to an organisation. Deming was the forefather who dispelled the idea that employees were costs to be minimised and nurtured a culture where associates should have the freedom to learn, fail, question and innovate.

'Deming believed everyone had a right to joy in work.'

The instructor went on to explain why they were ranked as one of the best places in the world to work with a human centred culture. Unlike other organisations they would all become stakeholders in the Park, they had no hierarchy, no layers of management just one elected central manager with a lattice of associates with equal responsibility to the team and the organisation.

The founders of the Park like W. L. Gore's founder Wilbert (Bill) L. Gore whose company never made a loss in over 50 + years believed that you can't have innovation without a shared vision in your business. If all our associates don't feel they are making a difference or feel valued we won't have collaboration or innovation. To be qualified as a leading associate in the Park would be determined by your peers and the followers you gain in the process of achieving both the Associates & Parks goals.

Finally the new recruits were introduced to a series of employee benefits unique to the Park; Remote-homework exchange program for individuals who were transitioning from maternity or parental or carers leave, their ongoing training programs of areas of professional interest to new recruits in developing their passions and personal visions for the future.

As Annie made her way to the other conservatories the instructor in the training room was delivering a role playing exercise. It was clear that the culture within the Park was one of organised structure yet the fundamental difference was that the associates were not being trained to be robots with parrot fashion scripts the systems and processes they were being shown and taught were guidelines to serving the customer with respect and courtesy. As each associate acted out different role playing exercises each individual brought their own personal character and style to the situation with the single objective of 'serving the customer'.

For Annie the culture displayed in the Human Resources room resonated with both her heart and her logic leaving her with the want to learn more of what the 'Black Box" tour had to teach her.

Chapter 7

II. The Manager; The Creation of a definite plan & purpose.

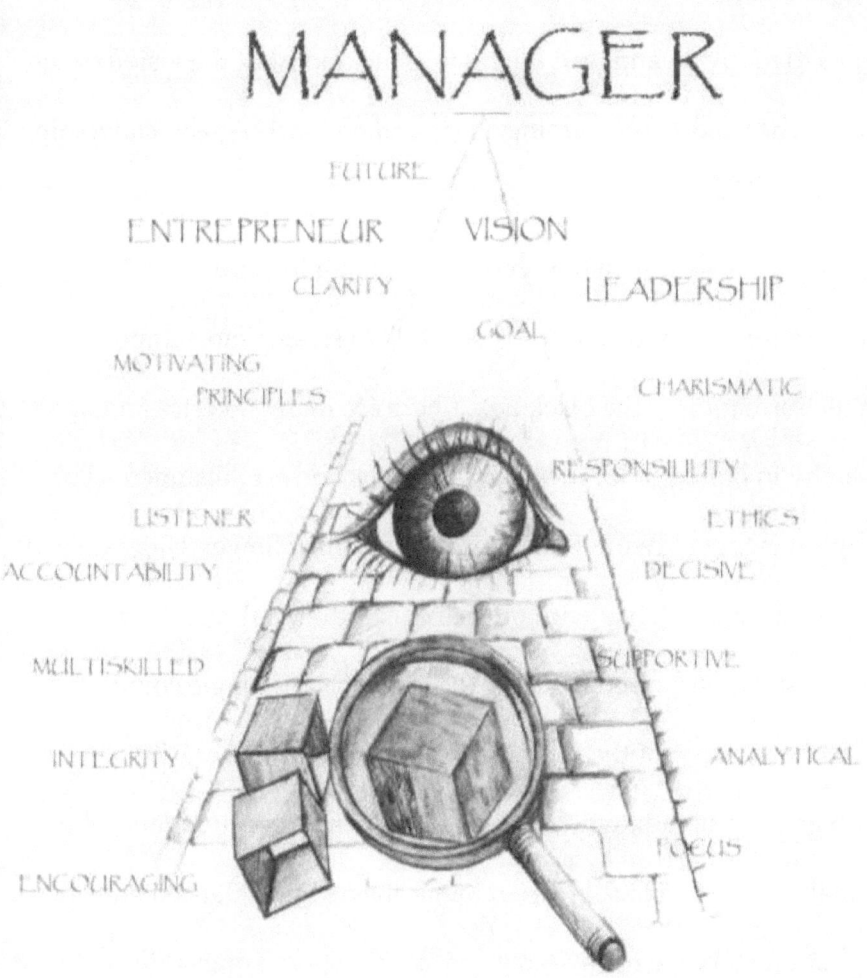

The Manager or more often known as the entrepreneur is the most important role of the black box. Without the manager there is no leadership, vision or focused plan or purpose for achieving anything. Every organisation needs a manger or leader and like operations without it everything turns into disorder and chaos. The good manager is an individual that has a diverse range of skills and knowledge and the attributes to motivate and lead others to share and fulfil the vision of the black box. The success of anything starts and ends with great leadership.

The Manager is essential in the preparation, planning and implementation of any plan or purpose. It is the single most important role in the formation of the black box. There are many theories and ideas of hierarchy in our communities, organisations and establishments but the simplest is that of two roles the leader and the follower. Ultimately we are all part of the black box with our various individual roles, functions and expertise synchronised together to achieving one single common goal. But the function of the leader is to ensure that the integrity of that common goal is pursued with clarity without prejudice or favour to any individual face of the black box to retain a strong and balanced enterprise. Throughout history we have seen examples where too many hierarchies destroy any sense of community and relationship with a detachment between the leader and the follower. Like wise this creates a chasm between our customers and the real world, with too many false hierarchies and leaders we become disassociated with our common purpose and goal.

Motivating personality

The most essential element of leadership is a 'motivating personality' ones energy, passion and self belief.

Many organisations make the wrong assumption that everyone has the skills and capacity to manage often rewarding individuals with the title based on their age or time served rather than assigning the role to an individual with a diversification of motivating people skills and an understanding of all sides of the black box. They often miss the fundamental point that if an enterprise succeeds it is because it starts and ends with good management.

Individual Responsibility& Ethics

It is the values that our managers 'demonstrate' rather than 'define' that will create how we are valued by our customers, staff and suppliers. When our operational principles are fulfilled through our actions then the black box principles gain their strength and stability. Principles must be demonstrated repeatedly as an ethos by its management for it ever to be absorbed by its work force and into the fabric of an enterprise.

Likewise our ability to motivate and recruit a work force starts with great leadership one that demonstrates cultural values which start with 'individual responsibility & ethics'. In all matters of human relations responsibility starts with the individual. Our will to take accountability and responsibility for our individual actions, choices and decisions will define our social and cultural standards and beliefs and the culture within our enterprises. A leadership with no value for individual responsibility or ethics will create and attract a work force and culture that lacks personal accountability, inequality and a legacy of resentment.

Decisive

The most obvious quality of a great manager is 'decisiveness'. In all matters of leadership it is essential that a leader has the ability to come to conclusions and decisions quickly clearly demonstrating his or her clear and definite purpose and the purpose of the black box. With a vision, plan and purpose decision making becomes very clear and simplified bringing speed to our decisions, actions and results. In all human relations the individual that demonstrates an ability to make quick decisions has a strong grasp of their spiritual and material purpose. This same quality will often take on a physical persona in ones physical stature, presence, speech and pace of movement and action. I have never met a man or woman whose success and achievement couldn't first be communicated by the first impression of their physical energy and presence.

Supportive & Encouraging

Many empires and enterprises have been built around exploitation, fear and dictatorship. Unfortunately this negative vibration finally rebounds on itself causing self destruction. The wise and learned have always favoured support and encouragement. The positive vibration of motivating others in the direction of pleasure as oppose to fear will propel single individuals to move mountains.

I have always profited from a leadership that builds rather than destroys. One can take the unlikeliest of characters and with some words of encouragement and belief you can create a great leader of industry. Like a child nurtured in a supportive and encouraging environment an encouraged employee will develop into a self reliant and confident individual.

Summary

I. Motivating personality

II. Individual Responsibility& Ethics

III. Decisive

IV. Supportive & encouraging

Chapter 8

The Leader

"The Creation of a definite plan & purpose."

Annie made her way to the second door way where she was instantly greeted by a warm and friendly mature woman, in an unfamiliar uniform. The woman exuded a poised calmness and modesty and immediately introduced herself with a firm handshake and a wide smile as 'Lauren' the Parks manager.

"Hi Annie I am delighted to meet you, a good friend of yours and mine told me that you would be joining us this evening and that you may enjoy some company on your tour, do you mind if I join you?" she asked sincerely.

"That would be brilliant" Annie replied nervously, pressing her hear-ring chip to silent mode.

Lauren led the way to the management doorway and invited Annie into a calm serene rectangular room sunken into the hillside surrounded by three pristine white walls and wall to wall dark wood flooring. The ceiling and far away wall were joined by two full panes of clear glass that faced an underground wall of white granite.

As the room was gently lit by the evening sky, the pitter-patter of rain rolled down the ceiling of glass gently cascading between the faraway wall of glass and white granite and like a gentle waterfall disappeared into the parks water recycling channels.

To my left the wall was filled with a mixture of old fashioned leather and paper back books next to a holograph shelf of 21st century books, films and publications. And to the right of the doorway we had entered sat a large white granite table embedded with five screens with live feeds from the other sectors. Behind the table the wall was filled with framed images of bygone entrepreneurs and leaders.

As I walked across the room the images changed with a second individual appearing in the background. Sir Alex Ferguson reappeared with his mentor Jock Stein, Walt Disney with his brother Roy Disney; Steve Jobs with his business partner Steve Wozniak, Bill Gore with his wife Vieve.

Lauren smiled at me amusingly and pointing at the images explained; 'The first lesson I ever learnt in business was that every great entrepreneur or manager has three important contributors to achieving their success, their mentor, their partner and their team. Behind every great individual there is;

I. A 'great mentor' and teacher who taught them the ropes gave them their apprenticeship in life or business and most likely gave them their first lucky break.

II. The 'partner' is most often the overlooked silent business partner who often goes unacknowledged possibly a spouse, brother or sister, personal assistant or confident.

III. And finally there are no great entrepreneurs, or managers without a 'team' of associates, people who share your passion and vision.

For me my greatest fascination in business has been discovering the story behind great entrepreneurs, their mentors, partners and associates.

Annie slowly scanned the faces of the individuals on the wall.

"Lauren, why do you think these individuals achieved such remarkable feats of success in their own area of expertise?' asked Annie.

"Call me old fashioned but I believe that the majority of people come to a point or junction in their life where they swap the wrongly perceived characteristics of the child for the adult. They relinquish their passion, belief, vision, idea's, values and will to take risks convinced they are simply childish thoughts. Where as each of these individuals choose to stay true to their beliefs and sought to pursue their dreams" said Lauren.

As I scanned the wall of real and holographic books I asked Lauren; 'So which is your favourite book and what would you recommend to an aspiring young entrepreneur?"

Without hesitation Lauren reached for one book an old hard back copy of 'Think and Grow Rich' by Napoleon Hill.

"This book without a shadow of a doubt is my favourite book for lots of reasons" Lauren said handing it to Annie.

"But for an aspiring entrepreneur wanting to learn something about the role of the Manager and Leadership I would recommend one of my books that resonates with real life, genuine old school management, something a fellow entrepreneur would recommend, let me see."

Searching the shelves Lauren finally found what she was looking for and took a copy of the legendary football manager Sir Alex Ferguson's book 'Leading' from the shelf and handed it to Annie.

Life may change and evolve over time but the simple principles of great leadership and management and people never change. You need someone with a definite plan and purpose, a motivating, supportive and encouraging personality. Most importantly a great manager takes accountability and individual responsibility for their decisions, and stands by their values and ethics.

This is a great book because the analogy of the football team is the same as a business. Great businesses are created by entrepreneurs, but to survive over time just like any football club you need to find a leader and manager who passionately believes in the vision and spirit of your club or business. Combine that with a great team or group of associates with the same shared vision and passion and you have a force to be reckoned with.

"I realise that the system within a football club doesn't have the complexity of what is required to design a nuclear submarine, build 50 million mobile phones or organise clinical trials for a new drug. But like every organisation we needed to be well run and had to be sure that our system was deeply ingrained. Our product just happened to be a football team, rather than a car or washing machine, and our whole reason for being was to make sure all the pieces of our product- all the different players- fitted together". Sir Alex Ferguson

"So how did you become the manager at the Worlds Creativity Park?" asked Annie?

"Well I fell in love with the place, I came here initially as a young teenager and like you wanted to be an entrepreneur and build my own business my own perfect black box. But once I started working here I realised I had found the perfect business for me a business that shared my values, ethics and my dreams. My passion and belief for this organisation drove me to win the respect of my associates. Here you are not promoted or rewarded for your age, who you know, what your qualifications are or just because you've been here a long time. Unlike other organisations you earn this position from the respect of your associates, and the contribution you make for the greater good for our customers, associates, suppliers and stakeholders."

I had a fabulous mentor who understood people, a veteran who had built their own business from the floor up not a theorist or a cog in a business. My mentor had a soft spot for young people and understood them, my story relates to a great quote of Sir Alex's;

'Youngsters can inject a fantastic spirit in an organisation and a youngster never forgets the person or organisation that gave him his (or hers) first big chance. He (she) will repay it with a loyalty that lasts

a lifetime. For young players nothing is impossible and they will try and run through a barbed-wire fence, while older players will try to find the gate'.

'Annie before we part company let me accompany you to my favourite sector' said Lauren.

At that Lauren led the way out of the Managers room and led the way to the next doorway. As they walked, Lauren extended to Annie the invitation to contact her when she would like to talk further or needed some friendly advice.

Chapter 9

III: Products or Services: Serving others with specialised knowledge or skills.

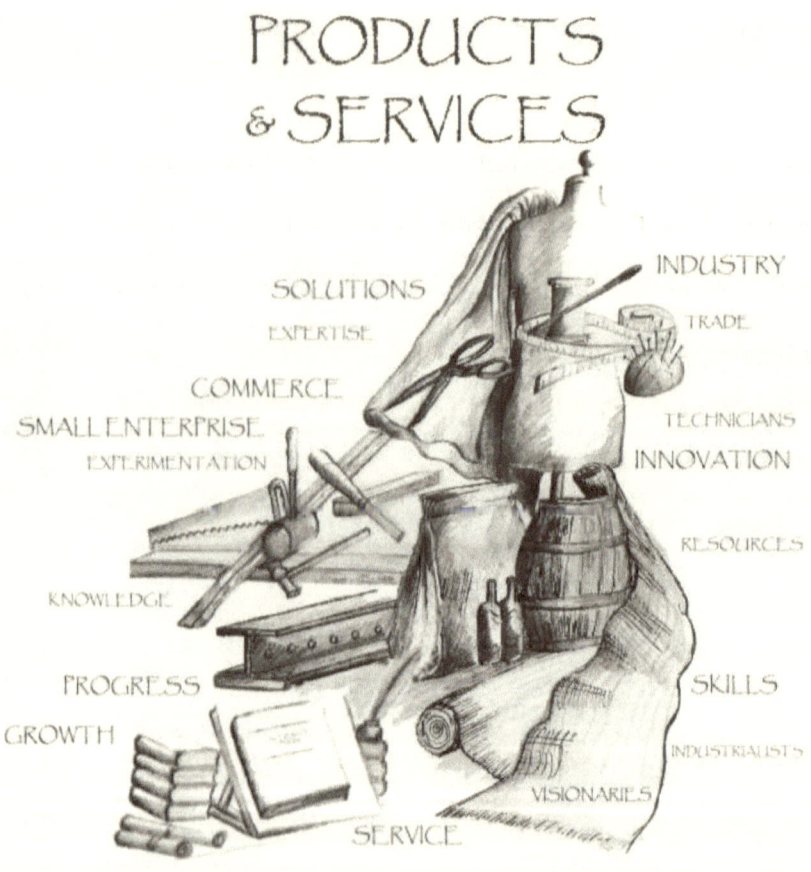

Life cannot progress or evolve without humanities motivation and need to grow, expand and evolve. The human condition to evolve comes from an individual's concentrated effort in developing their interest, knowledge and skill in a single area of expertise and sharing that expertise to serve and benefit humanity. Since the beginning of civilisation mankind has had an instinctive motivation to progress and evolve utilising the skills and resources of their environment on every continent of the world. The greater diversity and uniqueness each of us can develop offers greatest hope to civilisation to explore and expand the realms of possibility and progress.

One must discover what we can create or provide service in, to serve humanity. Through the centuries each nation has flourished through the single minded pursuit and commitment of individuals to master an area of specialised skill & knowledge developing new industries with our natural resources and materials. Nations from the Egyptians, Greeks to the Romans have either succeeded or failed as powerful rulers on the basis of the expertise of their engineers, mathematicians and thinkers. The more diverse our appreciation is for differing interests, areas of skill, knowledge and expertise the more equipped we will be to evolve and remain leaders in commerce, industry and development.

Great success comes from specialised skill or knowledge

We can create balanced and diverse economies capable of weathering all financial seasons if we govern our economies, education system and thinking to equate equal value and merit in all areas of expertise and skill. Many cultures have self destructed from not protecting essential elements for self sufficiency surrendering their interests in the industries of thinking, making or serving. No one has a magic ball to predict the emerging economies of the future but common sense can anticipate the basics we must protect for self sufficiency and survival through unpredicted storms.

Our care as custodians will be reflected in future generations.

Remember for those of us who are the caretakers of the next generation of mothers, fathers, grandparents, guardians and teachers we have a responsibility to help our children discover their source of self confidence and their material purpose and specialised skill. In their hands and minds lie our capacity to be the future leaders, industrialists, entrepreneurs and economists.

Our attentiveness and commitment to find within our resources the means for our children to develop and practice a chosen skill or area of knowledge as early as possible in their development will compound their level of self confidence and self reliance as adults. Our capacity to support and listen to our children's aspirations will be self evident in their decisiveness to choose a path in life as adults.

We all have individual strengths and weaknesses, our aptitude to either serve or produce must be given an environment to be valued, nurtured and grown. The mistake of many societies has been in their arrogance to portion value to thinking and studying over creating and caring, creating a society that places academia, science and medicine on a higher pedestal. We have a responsibility to start by providing our children with environments supportive and inclusive of all skills, abilities, aptitudes and interests if we wish to develop a more diverse society of skills and expertise.

Ones material purpose is a black box function providing a specific focused goal that will provide the financial rewards to care for us and our dependant's material needs in this physical world. Individuals can achieve this under the hospice and control of an employer. But history has always shown that no man or woman has gained greater personal reward than under the control of their own enterprise in the exchange of an innovative or specialised product or service. Owning your own enterprise is one of the most significant means of personal freedom, power and flexibility. It is also one of the most single means to find acceptability amongst every class. It gives an individual raised confidence, self respect, purpose, courage and clarity in defining ones material purpose in life. Small enterprises have always been the most powerful individual influences within any social structure and economy.

Small enterprise is the single most effective source for reaping the rewards of your labour & effort.

People often overlook the benefits of the small enterprise; the potential to design a template or model of enterprise to fulfil one's 'material purpose' with freedom and autonomy. By design its size encourages a sense of community and team work and a platform for individuality to flourish. Although it may be limited in resources or capital it often has the greatest capacity to evolve and succeed due to the additional commitment and effort it leverages from the sense of personal ownership of its workforce. The Small enterprise is the foundation and starting point for all great success in enterprise, a starting block often marginalised and unappreciated or celebrated by traditional educational and academic establishments.

It is the greatest builders of communities due to its foundations of a workforce being often cemented by generations of families and communities which pass on their precious skills, expertise and life experiences from one generation to the next. The children of these families and communities often receive a very unique and early education in life starting with the real life stories of enterprise depicted in their parents and grand parent's lessons of sacrifice, challenge, strife and success. Many start with a very early taste and introduction to labour and hard work working in the family business and an un-credited but early certification in the education and mechanics of enterprise, skill and hard work well before any of their peers or academic counterparts. Skills and knowledge that cannot be found in books or academic establishments but passed down from one generation to the next as real life stories fashioned as adventures and told at the dinner table to inspire a new generation of small enterprises.

Find inspiration in seeking to provide solutions.

All great achievement has come from humanities motivation to move towards love & pleasure or away from fear & pain and harnessing its motivation to inspire ideas to enhance and develop our society. An awareness of our societies' frustrations and nuisances are as important as our seeking of new pleasure and increased comfort. The individuals whom through history have received greatest material reward are those who have pursued the creation or of an innovation or a product or service that provides a solution to resolve the pain or pleasure of the day.

The close proximity of the small enterprise to the lay person as oppose to the hierarchies of the great establishments often offers the small enterprise greatest advantage to respond to these emerging needs with their personal commitment, specialised skills developed over generations and their speed and flexibility to respond and evolve. Providing solutions to humanities needs or frustrations is equally if not more important than improving profitability through financial or operational efficiencies. It will leverage increased customer loyalty, confidence and interest in your extended business offerings.

Focus on areas of Growth

Solving frustrations must be paired with the discernment to understand the difference between short term trends which meet the fleeting impulses and desires of the few with little substance or value or impact on economic growth. No matter what title or name you give it, cultures which become obsessed with 'illusion' over substance will eventually pay a heavy price for their lack of substance. The word illusion will take many names and guises but ultimately will hide inadequacy, laziness and stagnation. Everyone can appreciate good taste and pleasant and appealing appearance but ultimately only a deep substance to what we provide in a product or service in the form of real solutions or progress will generate economic growth. If a product or service cannot stand itself like all the other black boxes without the bells and whistles then we are regressing not progressing.

We must focus on understanding the products or solutions which bring meaningful long term growth prosperity and sustainability and cultural change. This is often found in improvements in efficiency, labour, material costs, time and speed. Economic growth has followed nations that embraced the development of new engineering and communication feats. The discernment of knowing the difference between fad and the future can propel a nation's growth as seen in mans inventions for conquering new lands from the creation of the wheel and shipping vessels to man's determination to conquer the air, land and sea.

Summary

I. Discover what you can create or provide service for to serve humanity.

II. Our care as custodians will be reflected in future generations.

III. Great success comes from specialised skill or knowledge

IV. Small enterprise is the single most effective source in receiving rewards for your labour and effort.

V. An Inspiring idea or purpose can be found in both humanities hopes and fear.

VI. Find inspiration in seeking to provide solutions.

VII. Focus on areas of Growth

Chapter 10

To Serve: Serving others with specialised knowledge or skills.

Annie and Lauren made their way along a long winding external tunnel of glass that looked out onto the West garden. The garden was subtly lit with a carpet of scattered solar lights that traced the shingle path in the garden like fireflies at dusk. In the distance a harr slowly appeared across the loch as darkness fell and a still calmness and tranquillity filled the Park. As they exited the tunnel Annie looked at Lauren slightly bemused to find herself in 'The Great Pioneers Hall'.

'Before you say anything, yes this serves as both our Products and Services sector and 'The Great Pioneers Hall'. What better place to get a true grasp of what our customer's frustrations and dreams are. Here our associates meet our customers personally every day. Unlike other organisations we are not detached from our customers. Here we listen, observe, interact, and subtly test and trial our new products and services.' said Lauren.

Annie proceeded along the red paved hall of fame with its 8 protruding exploration pods that lined each side of the tunnel. For the first time in her life she experienced the Park without the company of hundreds of other guest's only associates.

Each pod had a small group of associates from a different sector and like small individual enterprises they utilised the workshop areas to discuss the day's findings. They took the feed back and observations they made of the public on how to improve the services in the Park along with the 'magical left over crumbs of ideas' for new products and innovations which they enthusiastically took back and developed in the 'Designovator's Room'.

Providing a good service was the easy part for the associates. Just like great organisations like 'Disney World' in Florida their continual analysis of their processes and procedures and the use of 'Kaizen' over the years had created a model 'to serve' that was the envy of every business owner. Our role in the Worlds Creativity Park is to be constantly reinventing the Park and being at the forefront of innovation. Having learnt the lesson of the early 21st century the constant challenge for the Park was to teach the next generation how to create new products, innovations and inventions. As an economy we no longer based everything on purely our service industry.

Like the Japanese after the 2nd World War who had to find something to sell to the world and enlisted the help of W. Edwards Deming to rebuild its country and economy. In 2020 the West and our economy in particular could no longer risk and depend sole on the service industry for 78% of our GDP.

Our associates challenge was to strike the balance of utilising their unique specialised skills and identifying and guiding our vision for the Park in areas of real potential growth. The associates deliberated on areas of growth from the comments, attitudes and opinions expressed by the youngest and eldest of their visitors. The associates observed their guests during workshops, and took inspiration from the solutions they suggested for prevailing concerns and frustrations in their daily lives. We built into our model the advice taken from the likes of Sam Walton founder of 'Wal-Mart'.

"...give more responsibility for making decisions to the people who are actually on the firing line, those who deal with the Customers everyday. Good management is going to start listening to the ideas of these line soldiers. Pooling these ideas and disseminating them around their organisations so people can act on them."

They modelled their thinking on the predictions of James Dyson and visionaries such as Elon Musk. Our fourth largest contributor to GDP was once North Sea gas and oil which had been changed for ever due to the innovations developed by one man and his companies Space-X, Tesla and Solar City. Elon Musk like many great visionaries was ridiculed by the establishment and as an outsider who dIdn't feel constricted by the establishments rules he proved them all wrong. He took his profits from one of his first businesses in the service industry namely Banking 'Paypal' and invested it in tangibles, products and innovation and the rest is history.'

I had visited 'The Great Pioneers Hall' so many times with my grandmother but for the first time I saw another dimension to what it was designed to achieve. I recalled how every time I visited the hall and visited a new pod an associate would provide an opportunity for me to try a new skill or role play in a different profession. They gave me my earliest experience of experimenting with new ideas like the great inventor Dyson.

'Lauren do you know what 'The Great Pioneers Hall' taught me as a little girl? It taught me not be afraid of failing or taking risks. But more importantly it prodded my imagination and gave me the permission to dream.' said Annie sincerely.

'There is a favourite quote of mine shared by the legendary Dame Anita Roddick founder of 'The Body Shop' which we aspire to as part of the philosophy shared by all our associates' said Lauren;

"My vision, my hope is simply this: that many business leaders will come to see a primary role of business as incubators of the human spirit, rather than factories for the production of more material goods & services."

Chapter 11

IV. Sales; Persistence and the understanding of human desires and fears.

From every continent North, South, East and West alongside the great adventurer and explorer is the master of people and persuasion the great travelling salesperson. One of the greatest art forms is the beguiling art and gift of selling whether the Romany gypsy foretelling your fortune to the merchant with his spices and silks. The wheels of enterprise will keep moving as long as you share the simple understanding of people and their motivations of desire or fear.

Mastering sales comes from a genuine interest in people and developing a repertoire of communication skills to mix among all class or group of individuals. It is an art of both listening and speaking mixed with a pleasing and amiable personality. It is often fused with an instant image and presence of enthusiasm and stature exhibited in ones body language, grooming and attire. It requires a resilient personality uninfluenced by rejection or temporary defeat and deep understanding of human desires and fears.

Desires

Man and woman's deepest desires keep the wheels of industry moving. With progress or innovation comes social change and new personal aspirations. The invention of the sewing machine and industrialisation of the cotton mills brought cheap cloth and clothing to the masses and the introduction of the insatiable desire for 'fashion' and a social revolution. The steel industry brought us ships, trains and railway links that expanded the potential to trade over frontiers and continents and the desire for cheaper and more ready available foods, minerals and materials i.e. Tea, coffee, sugar cane to cotton. Every great sales person understands that being on the crest of the wave of the latest new desire of the masses gives them greatest advantage to sell their wears.

Man and woman's need to socially conform and acquire the same material trappings as their peers or social group is instinctive. The gift of a great sales person is their people and communication skills that adapts to every new customer intuitively pin pointing ones tendency towards desire or motivation away from fear. The analytical sales person will perfect their trade to mirror the behaviour of their customer and naturally align their thinking to identify your fundamental motivations and desires to package and deliver a product or service that meets your needs. They will stack up benefits and values like a wish list of promising rewards.

Fears

Fear is an equally powerful driving force as desire. Some of us are motivated by the attainment of our desires and the rest of us by the avoidance of that which we fear most; the loss of finances, material objects, pride or love. The institutions that promote security, safety and protection survive and prosper on humanities simplest fears, loss of home, health, material possessions and life and promise of the afterlife. The perceived moral and righteous establishments govern as moral authorities protecting your interests and well being from bankers, lawyers, insurers and governments to religious leaders.

Humans need to be accepted, belong and conform is one of the most motivating forces of enterprise. The fear of exclusion is a powerful motivation in our behaviours to buy and collect material possessions of various forms. From our perceived class, working role or profession to how this is demonstrated to the world by where we live and the objects we outwardly own and exhibit. The beguiling art and gift of selling will provide answers to solving or quashing your fears with the latest product or service that meets your need.

Art of persuasion

The great sales person cannot motivate by 'desire & fear' alone. As mentioned previously enterprises built on lies and 'illusion' will only sustain a short shelf life through their complacency and lack of progress. Enterprises meet the test of time with an offering of substance, quality and innovation. The most persuasive sales person will find selling much simpler with a product or service they deem 'genuine' that resonates with their values.

Beyond this you can sell sand to the Arabs if you invest in a good product or service with benefits and qualities that exceed the competition. The combined personality of the entrepreneur and sales person is a powerful force where one is the creator and driving force for the vision of a product or service.

Persistance

The single characteristic of the sales person is the skill and mastery of persistence. Persistence is the quality of one with a 'definiteness of purpose and vision'. With clarity and vision you will overcome temporary defeat and stay firm to the path you have chosen. Through out history the great conquerors, adventurers and explorers have shared this same attribute. Without persistence opportunity is lost at the first hurdle and is replaced with failure.

Persistence is a quality often acquired through the experience of temporary defeat and failure and even a short period of disillusionment and despondency. It is often mastered when one has sacrificed and lost almost everything with nothing more left to loose before rebounding to fight the final battle to achieve ones goal and purpose.

Summary

I. Desires

II. Fears

III. Art of Persuasion

IV. Persistence

Chapter 12

The Sales Person; Persistence and the understanding of human desires and fears.

Annie proceeded on her tour alone, and stood peering across the vast under ground cavern as everyone busily went about their work. She reflected on what lessons she had learnt about the first three sides of the 'black box' and the functions of building a business of her own.

As she stood thinking about all those great quotes and revered entrepreneurs and leaders she still couldn't help looking down at her leather bound book with its letters thinking of Mary with equal awe and respect. Annie wondered whether society really understood the accumulative significance of all those unknown millions of one person businesses many with the modest goal of creating a better life for them selves and their families. Many individuals just like Mary, which were the back bone of our communities and economies with a purpose equally significant to those remembered and studied in our history books, colleges and universities.

Annie recalled vividly her favourite story about Mary and her first enterprise during the Second World War. Mary had acquired a small allotment where she grew vegetables and raised chickens for their eggs to gain an income and make ends meet. One morning Mary had arrived at the allotment to find that a fox had killed all but one of her chickens. But as usual never to be defeated in business, Mary promptly gathered up all the dead chickens placed them in a potato sack and briskly headed home. Entering her kitchen Mary quickly cleared the kitchen table and took one chicken at a time and laid them out for inspection, carefully removing any eggs that could be salvaged that had not yet been laid, washing them and placing them in a basket.

Without hesitation she then proceeded to pluck and clean every chicken that could be salvaged for meat or stock. With fresh white meat and eggs on strict rationing she sent a message round the neighbour hood to all her neighbours that Mary Burns had chickens and eggs for sale. Within an hour she had a queue at her back door and by lunch time the money in her pocket to replace all of her dead chickens with her enterprise back on the road.

Annie loved Mary's stories for they revealed a stark contrast between the theories of all those business advisors, consultants and academics and the harsh truth of her real life experiences and the challenges of entrepreneurship.

With increased clarity Annie briskly made her way to the doorway and elevator to the 'Sales' sector continuing her lessons in mastering the six functions of business. As Annie entered the elevator the re-engineered transcript from Sam Walton's book 'Made in America' (founder of 'Wal-Mart') was replayed from the 1990's.

"...a lot of folks ask me **two** related questions all the time. The first one is could a Wal-Mart type story still occur in this day and age? My answer is of course it could happen again. Somewhere out there right now there's someone-probably hundreds of thousands of some ones-with good enough ideas to go all the way. It will be done again, over and over, providing that someone wants it badly enough to do what it takes to get there. It's all a matter of attitude and the capacity to constantly study and question the **management of the business.**"

Annie listened intently.

".... The second question is if I were a young man or woman starting out today with the same sorts of talents and energies and aspirations that I had fifty years ago, what would I do? That answer to that is a

*little harder to figure out, I don't know exactly what I would do today, but I feel pretty sure **I would be selling something**……….."*

At that the elevator doors opened and Annie entered a brightly lit lecture theatre where a lively sales presentation was being given by a short immaculately dressed gentleman. As Annie entered the room the gentleman briskly approached her introducing himself as Desmond with a warm smile and a handshake. With his own charismatic manner Desmond introduced Annie to his audience as his guest like an old uncle welcoming her into his home.

As Desmond continued his presentation the 20 trainees stood attentively perched against their high stools that evenly surrounded the lecturing platform;

"Unlike conventional businesses we have the great pleasure at the Worlds Creativity Park of having an exceptionally refined product and service which comes close to quite literally 'selling itself'. Yes 'selling' is fundamental to our business, we have our sales associates who specialise in 'Sales training' but unlike conventional business's every associate has the shared role and responsibility of being part of our sales force. We do not discriminate between the different functions and sectors of our business and therefore there are no preferential bonuses, wages and commissions assigned to a sales department and a designated sales team. As associates our collective efforts are rewarded equally through our stocks, shares and wages. We have discovered that our profitability as a company is directly linked to sales driven by associates who are genuinely passionate about our product and service not 'sales people on commission who would sell anything to their Granny'."

Desmond continued to demonstrate that every role within the Park had a sales function whether you were the cleaner, the security guard, the manager or accounts clerk. He discussed the importance of utilising their listening skills and every form of nonverbal, verbal and visual 'communication' to understand each customer, how to mirror and match customer behaviour. In Desmond's humorous manner he demonstrated how a simple nonverbal nod, smile or even wink could engage a child or adult and begin building customer rapport.

He spent some time discussing various sales training techniques, basics in selling and customer service. Followed by a brief talk on the importance of genuinely valuing the customer with common courtesies i.e. good morning, good night, thank you, please, simple gems like remembering someone's name. After a rigorous and detailed presentation with role playing and exercises Desmond finally closed the presentation with an open question session. From the front of the audience a young trainee associate asked;

"Why do you not have a sector for marketing?"

"Well if I take you back 40 years ago, business was so deluded by "marketing" and advertising that we forgot how to build 'real' sustainable businesses with quality products and services with value and growth. We became obsessed as a country with building what they called 'brand names'. Marketing was tarnished by becoming a false function of business that was used to mask and deflect from business's that were unsustainable and simply about poor goods and consumption.

Many companies mistook marketing for one of the six sides of the black box rather than what it really is simply packaging, wrapping paper and the frill you add to the outside of a business after you have designed, engineered and built an intelligent business model. Yes of course Marketing has its place in every Business but it if you have a world class product or service like us, like Dyson, Disney etc. *the real Marketing team you reward are your associates, while your customers will provide the service for 'FREE'.*"

From the back of the audience an older trainee raised her hand;

"Hi Desmond, why do the trainers repeatedly ask us whether we have a genuine *passion* and *belief* for what you do here? "

"Well that's simple if your answer is 'yes' then congratulations we have completed the first and most important test to identifying if you qualify to become a *new associate*, we can provide the rest!" said Desmond.

Chapter 13

V. Finance; Material wealth through the mastery of financial education

Finance like the six sides of the Black box can be understood and mastered with a little discipline and commitment. No one is too young to master its teachings and principles all one needs is the basic skills to read, write and count. Financial wisdom starts with a few simple principles and grows with the commitment to learn more as the world of finance evolves and innovates. The ability to develop the skills of discerning between sound financial advice and logic is essential to obtain the full benefits of a financial education. A financial education will reap long term personal wealth, economic success and security for you, your family & community.

Become a master of finances and economics

Throughout the centuries financial mastery is a subject often disguised to appear complicated and confusing, to allow the privileged to manipulate power and fear over the uneducated. Secret misconceptions and beliefs have been created about wealth throughout history to simply enslave the many and free the few. Many answers to financial mastery are still preserved in our emotional mastery and control of our financial decisions and impulses.

Those who discipline themselves in a financial education will protect and increase their fortunes, understanding how the wealthy acquire, grow and protect their wealth. How through history and across all continents governments have created systems for rewarding the financially educated and wealthy through tax systems on income, property and assets. They will learn the lessons of history and the importance of knowing when things are least or most valuable as assets and forms of tender i.e. precious metals, coins, paper money or modern currency. They come to learn how our economies work and operate and how understanding even the simplest principles i.e. saving, interest, compound interest, inflation, investments etc. can change their relationship with money.

Men and women have lost fortunes through the centuries by passing ownership of their financial decisions to others. Many of us allow our government, employer, spouse, business partner or financial advisors to make the most important of all our financial decisions. Financial mastery is not exclusive to the wealthy we all possess the single essential tool for financial mastery.

The single difference between the masters of finance and the normal lay person is that financial masters make their decisions with their 'brain' and the normal lay person by their emotions and their 'heart'. Through the centuries the poor have been enslaved by their emotional attachment to money. Emotions connected to the fear of poverty, a deep rooted lack of ignorance on the subject and the egos lack of discernment.

The wealthiest individuals in history have taken control of their financial thinking and committed to studying, reading or taking lessons each calendar month on the subject of finance and economics. You know you are on the right path when you learn to disconnect your emotions to money and replace the connection with logic and knowledge. Once you are aware of your emotional connections to money you will be much more equipped to make logical and rational decisions and one step away from no longer being a slave to money.

Master financial education and money will become your servant

Our ability to generate wealth is limited by the efficiency of our tools, the value of our individual skilled labour, expertise and education are restricted by the individual hours we can perform in a day, week, or month as servants to money. The most efficient means long term to creating wealth and security will not always be from you or your employee's labour but through educating yourself sufficiently to understand what makes money grow, making money your servant and you its master.

The greatest obstacle to a financial education and taming money to become your servant is your own negative personal relationships and connections with money. If you obtain a full working knowledge of finance you will ultimately destroy your fears. Take time to search out and listen to the wealthy, rich, wise financial elders and study financial history, books on entrepreneurs and economists.

Learn to discern between needs and wants.

Secondly to master money one must change our emotional connections starting by discerning between needs and wants. An individual can come from poverty and build wealth from a great career and enterprise. But too often the poor person's misperception about wealth believes that this means having everything; the displays of material goods, the bigger lifestyle, the persona and image of perceived wealth. The financially educated understand that financial security and wealth is built on discerning between needs and wants and using your surplus earnings to invest in your future without this wealth will only be temporary.

Without this our lives will become harder as we become consumed as servants working for money. If one can adopt the lifestyle of needs not wants one will begin to accumulate the resources to save and invest in building our financial future. This is the first step to financial freedom by learning to live within our means. This is one of the simplest lessons which when mastered can offer an individual greatest emotional release from the "fear" of money and provide a new sense of self empowerment. It is an essential lesson valued and practiced by the most successful of entrepreneurs, a lesson often learnt early in the inception of an enterprise and if practiced will help build a valuable enterprise of assets not liabilities.

Learn to discern between assets and liabilities.

Hand in hand with learning to discern between needs and wants is recognising the difference between assets and liabilities. To ultimately be free of money and no longer be its slave we must look at developing assets and means of converting our money and savings into our servant. Then our lives can weather the good and bad times providing strong foundations and platform to build our financial future and securities. One must change ones focus both personally and in business to the simple question of assets and liabilities.

I. An asset is a purchase which will increase your wealth & add to your financial income every calendar month.
II. A liability is a purchase which will reduce your wealth & add to your financial expenses every calendar month.

Ones focus must be to build assets that you need, not liabilities that reduce your wealth and are simply impulsive wants that add to monthly expenses and living costs. An asset can be as simple as a carpenter's tool or a fisher mans rod enabling one to make a living to a self generating asset like a piece of property or business which brings you a small consistent and profitable rent or income every month.

Only begin building your financial assets once you have created a reliable emergency fund for lives unexpected difficulties and challenges from loss of property, security, health or employment.

One can begin to feel the empowerment of financial education when one has acquired enough assets and savings that they become your labourers and provide an income every month to pay for the liabilities we need to live. The wealthy ensure every one of their labourers is serving them efficiently by being their own book keeper or a tight overseer of all their financial decisions and judgements.

Be your own book keeper

A good book keeper will focus on income producing assets that give you cash flow and money in your pocket from: property, shares, bonds, commodities, business or art. And not liabilities that take money out of your pocket: bigger home, more expensive food or clothing.

A good book keeper is an effective negotiator and buyer able to discern between emerging trends and fads and financially skilled in investing in areas of personal interest or areas they possess specialised expertise. They are sufficiently educated to take risks based on solid facts, estimations and forecasts and will always be free from personal debt.

Being a good book keeper is like the simple disciplines and principles of taking care of your health, exercise, and diet keeping your body in good physical shape. You need to learn good habits early as a child learning always to pay attention to the small print, taking care of the pennies that in turn take care of the pounds, how to budget, save and invest. Being sufficiently educated prepares you for adulthood by taking responsibility for defining your own long term financial vision and plan and understanding the basic fundamentals from tax entitlements to taking care of your wealth with the appropriate forms of insurance.

Build your Financial Portfolio in your area of expertise.

As a good book keeper you are then well prepared to intelligently build your own financial portfolio. A good financial portfolio is a well defined plan for achieving your financial goals through means relative to your individual areas of expertise whether its Business, Property, Stocks, Bonds or Intellectual Property with diversified risks that are always insured and protected. Define your financial goals and invest your savings in areas you have the greatest level of expertise and knowledge reducing any vulnerability to risk. Define your personal time lines that you need to maximise your financial payouts and returns to ultimately provide you with a sufficient income to sustain your life style free from labour.

Financial timing

'Financial timing' is crucial to all issues of financial mastery from knowing strategically when to buy or sell to understanding economic seasons. Mastering financial timing can compound your financial assets in one single decision with the timing of when to both purchase and then in turn sell property, business or major investment.

The skill in financial timing must be combined with specialised knowledge and your understanding of a subject or market i.e. property, art, antiques, business's. Every great financial house or family throughout history have benefited repeatedly from a clear understanding of this single skill. As stated earlier the nature of life is ever changing in cycles of both fortune and misfortune, but neither is ever constant our economies are like the seasons of the year and the cycles of new life and growth, with our financial seasons rotating over a decade rather than a 12 calendar month.

We must learn to discern which season we are currently in and anticipate and prepare for the coming seasons. As individuals we have a life spanning four seasons our Childhood, Youth, Adulthood and Old age. The wise teach their children early about the habit of saving and the secrets of 'compound interest', their youth understand that it will not always be 'summer' so invest for those rainy days. This same principle applies to our economies nothing ever stays the same and like nature we have our spring, summer, autumn and winter with differing rewards, challenges and demands.

Spring: Like the farmers we sew our seeds, planning and preparing for extra labourers and managing our flow of money.

Summer: We harvest our crops, spending our profits and expand with new equipment, the hiring of new farm hands; we enjoy life and a little extravagance.

Autumn: We do our housekeeping, we get rid of dead wood reduce our costs, repair our equipment and buildings. We prepare for the downturn and look after what we have.

Winter: We look after what we have, trim back on our labourers save the pennies and the pounds we look after our existing customers. We tighten our cash flow and buy up- cheap bargains, reducing our overheads, getting back to basics.

It is important to keep a perspective of the natural cycles of life and like our lives economies and business is not free from the good times or bad.

Summary

I. Become a master of finances and economics

II. The brain is the single essential tool in financial mastery.

III. Master financial education and money will become your servant

IV. Learn to discern between needs and wants.

V. Learn to discern between assets and liabilities.

VI. Be your own book keeper

VII. Build your Financial Portfolio in your area of Expertise

VIII. Financial Timing

Chapter 14

The Book Keeper: Material wealth through the mastery of financial education.

As Annie approached the threshold of the Finance sector the facial recognition cameras registered her identity, approving her clearance and access to the financial centre of the Park. As she stepped forward to the glass of the security doors she noticed a single quote engraved into the glass;

"No society can surely be flourishing and happy of which the far greater part of the members are poor and miserable" Adam Smith

At that the door slid open and its sensors triggered the lighting system, illuminating the floor of the darkened room. As Annie entered the tiny circular room of glass a computer generated voice of a woman invited her to have a seat in the large cushioned chair positioned in the centre of the room. As Annie sat down the glass doors closed behind her and the room returned to darkness as the glass in front of her transformed into an array of moving green letters and numbers. Within seconds five smaller screens appeared side by side behind the glass with muted live video feeds from each of the other 5 sectors with a conference meeting discussing the stats on the day's income and expenditure.

As all the associates spoke, a series of reports appeared on the screen of the Parks financials, dissected by; time, location, associate, venue, customer demographic. The output of statistical data was overwhelming and the minute incremental differences recorded were bewildering with sales comparisons measured against comparative years, months factoring in comparative data including seasonal variants, weather conditions, and traffic to staff absenteeism.

As the Parks finance team continued their live feed, the computer spoke once more and introduced itself as the Book Keeper or 'BK'. A second screen then appeared with a short film accompanying the computers monologue explaining the background operations and model of the finance sector and its revolutionary system.

"Good Evening, Welcome to our Accounts Centre, this sector is different to every other section of our organisation being a fully automated and computerised process with only 1% external input from financial associates and auditors. Our system was developed at the inception of the

Park and represents one of the most pioneering inventions and valuable IP assets of our organisation becoming a business model independent of the external banking system and manual accounting process.

After establishing a unique partnership with world businesses; in an exchange program that gave them commercial access to our technology and unique software algorithm, we were able to achieve our vision of becoming a cashless and banker free society. With our company policy to share all Intellectual Property with the general public our unique software was made public as a charitable entity in 2020 allowing everyone to be their own personal bank.

This included the equivalent of your own personal financial advisor a 'Spell Checker' for finances that advised how to correct poor financial decision making and planning. With the development and implementation of a unique international coding system in 2022 that identified every product sold or purchased in the world we were able to provide an accounting process that registered each transaction electronically in real time to every individual, household or business using our lifetime free software."

As 'BK' spoke a different pie chart and histogram appeared on the screen demonstrating the incremental impact from the use of its software and the improvement in financial education.

"Since 2025 individual personal investments into long term saving has increased by 23%, money laundering, corporate and individual tax evasion has been reduced by 72%, national personal debt has decreased by 32% with an increase of 25% in first time buyers purchasing their own home. The sustainability and mortality rate of small businesses, in particular sole traders with no employees has improved dramatically. In 2013 by year 3 only 6 out of every 10 businesses survived now we have 10 out of every 10. At year 5 instead of only 4 of 10 businesses surviving we have 9. In 2065 instead of only <u>1 business surviving at year 10</u> we have 8 of every original 10 business start-ups not only surviving but also employing 5 or more associates."

The computer continued by asking Annie did she have any questions she would like to ask, stating that it was programmed to answer over 3 million questions that would be anticipated by tour guests visiting the finance sector related to economics, finance and business.

Annie sat for a moment and thought carefully before answering;

"What is the 1% input that the associates and auditors have to the system?"

"Our software program operates in tandem with the legal parameters of the law and economics i.e. tax, vat, hourly rates, interest rates etc. which is fully accessible to auditors. Each individual software program has 1% of its system determined by what we call the 'emotional' profile of its user determining; selective purchasing, profit margins, resale price to the customer, charitable contributions, staff contributions i.e. shares, stocks and bonuses. Ultimately this 1% determines the individual moral and ethical values of an organisation and its impact on determining the relationship it develops with its customer, staff, suppliers and the wider community."

"I have one last question I would like to ask…… What do you define as the secret to financial success?" said Annie.

"Simple Financial Education" said BK.

With that Annie stood up and as she waited for the glass doors to open she noticed the words engraved at her feet across the threshold of the door; "Every man lives by exchanging".

Chapter 15

VI. Operations; The power & orchestration of organised systems, processes & people.

'Operational' mastery is the glue that keeps the black box together. The black box is about order, discipline and consistency. Without logical processes, habits and rules everything becomes chaos. It is an essential element of the black box without which everything would collapse and cease to function. The man or woman whom masters the power & control of orchestration of organised systems, processes & people will benefit from one of lives most precious assets 'time'.

The organised minds of great nations like the Romans have propelled human evolution and society through their organised thinking, time saving solutions and the orchestration of people, skills and resources. Their development and execution and vision for Europe were self evident in the legacy of the infrastructure of their roads, bridges, waste and water systems impacting directly on the economic power of individual nations. Operational mastery has the potential to increase your momentum and speed to achieving your social and economic goals as an individual, organisation or nation.

Develop an Organised Mind

The organised mind can create order out of chaos. All great masters of trades or crafts develop a natural appreciation for logic and order allowing them to perfect and improve their skills and share their knowledge methodically with their apprentices and students. If you visit the studio of any great artist or crafts person you will discover an array of tools and materials carefully and strategically organised.

The development of an organised mind is essential in supporting the most essential principle of the black box discovering ones single material purpose in life. With an organised mind one can focus and organise ones efforts to work strategically and efficiently to form a plan in reaching ones ultimate goal. In chaos our efforts and speed are thwarted in reaching the finishing line first and winning competitive advantage over our opponents or competition.

Like wise the developed rules of law and order, ethics and morality all hinge on the human condition and need for common shared values and rules without which everything would transform into chaos and anarchy. Without order it is impossible to measure progress, success or failure. Operational mastery is necessary if only to measure time, productivity, profitability and customer value. Any enterprise without operational mastery will hinder its ability and speed of growth because it interlinks with every component and side of the black box.

Time the new gold.

Time doesn't discriminate it has no master it is a commodity and asset that we all have of equal measure whether we are rich or poor, young or old. Unfortunately time only has a 24 hr shelf life which we cannot buy any more of at the end of the day or store away for a rainy day. Some of us spend it aimlessly without thought or intention. Others grasp it so tight that we forget how to embrace and enjoy it, before long Time will become the new gold.

As we have evolved through the ages we have developed new time saving devices and inventions yet still can't find enough hours in the day. The more civilisation progresses the less time we will have both in our personal and working lives. The rapid speed of modernisation and industrialisation has made time a precious and scarce commodity that we all wish we had more of. An organised mind understands that systems and processes measure the efficiency of our time and offer some solutions for improvement. The organised mind values this commodity, focusing on investing it rather than spending it, knowing that we must act now as this minute, hour or day will not come again.

Invest your time don't spend it.

Productivity comes from the organised person who finds new ways and solutions of reducing wasted resources and unnecessary repetition. An awareness of new innovations, tools and discoveries is essential to the improvements in productivity. The simple introduction of a tool such as the loom or sewing machine revolutionised the textile industry and changed our capacity and vision in the supply of textiles and clothing like so many other industries. Finding new tools that leverage greatest benefit from our efforts, skill and time are essential to productivity. Unfortunately many generations have preferred to leverage productivity through the exploitation of others labour rather than the noble pursuit of expanding the potential products of their minds. For this very reason those with organised minds have built their careers and fortunes in the pursuit of time saving solutions and innovations in particular in the pursuit of careers where you;

Work once and get paid forever.

The organised mind values 'wisdom' above all attributes and skills and consistently searches for new solutions to improve efficiency. That is why it understands the financial benefits of 'working once and getting paid forever' through intellectual property; licensing, patents, inventions or copyright creating books, scripts etc. The organised mind will never be penniless because they are always searching for new solutions and means to improving efficiency and profitability and means to acquiring self generating assets.

Individuals whom understand the laws and principles of our financial institutions and governments know they are designed to benefit the wealthy and educated. There are many penniless composers, musicians, play rights, poets and authors to inventors, thinkers and scientists whose lives passed without financial reward having lacking the knowledge of gaining legal ownership and protection for their ideas and works. Great empires, individual and family wealth has been built on self generating assets of land, property and legal ownership of new ideas.

Measure everything

To fully execute the power & control of orchestration of organised systems, processes & people we must finally find a means of measuring everything. Without a means to measure all our resources and efforts we cannot define success or failure, progress or improvement. It is essential that within every function of our enterprise or organisation we have the ability to calculate all increments of time, labour and resources. The analytical element of operational mastery is essential to maintain healthy competition and a value of how the little things influence the bigger picture.

Find your own unique operational strength

To fully utilise the power of operations it is necessary that one of the most important core functions of one or two sides of the box are operationally more intelligent and smarter than your competitors or adversaries. If you wish to outwit your competition you must think smarter and shrewder in either your Product or service, Management, Human Resources, Finance or Operations.

The answer to this can often be found in new innovation, technology, resources, cultural changes or needs. Often the easiest common denominator is Finances either in the reduction of material, product, time or labour costs. But those who can look beyond conventional thinking and combine it with operational wisdom will always find a better way.

The Price to pay

Ultimately every reward in life comes with a personal price to pay; our time, money or labour. The individual that fully masters the power and orchestration of organised systems, processes and peoples will understand that the operations side of the black box is the only side of the box which will control and reduce that price you pay. Operational mastery can help you design a model of life and business that will protect that which you value most and dearest.

Summary

I. Develop an Organised Mind

II. Time the new gold

III. Invest your time don't spend it.

IV. Work once and get paid forever

V. Measure everything

VI. The Price to pay

Chapter 16

The Analyst; The power & orchestration of organised systems, processes & people.

As Annie approached the last doorway she reflected on a comment her Gran had made, telling her to pay particular attention to what she observed in the operations sector the place that promoted *'working on the business not in the business'* there lay the secret of what enabled her to design a business and operating system which protected what she personally valued most, 'time'. For Gran this allowed her to prioritise her role and responsibilities as a parent and give her the freedom to also pursue building a business. A lesson many business owners failed to ever learn.

Entering the last sector and inside the large circular Operations room Annie looked down from a raised external viewing platform that encircled the room. Below a large wooden table filled the centre of the room with seats positioned evenly around its circumference one assigned to each sector of the park. On the table in front of each seat balanced the latest state of the art 4-D plasma ball monitor on a silver balancing platform.

As Annie watched associates come and go, she recognised the group of associates she had previously saw in the Products and Services sector. She watched as they spoke with the analyst seated at the desk discussing observations made from today's interactions with their customer's and how these could be applied as operational improvements.

The plasma balls looked like giant electronic spheres with multiple veins connecting from various angles and leading off in different directions. On closer inspection as the analyst magnified a section more closely one could identify images connecting a group of folders with an individual symbol or colour denoting a saving in time, energy, finances etc.

The analyst's appeared to have a real grasp of the workings of the Park an almost visionary perspective. The speed with which they were able to identify existing protocols or processes in the Park appeared like the behaviour of a master craftsperson with an intricate understanding of the mechanics and workings of their product, continually refining and perfecting their masterpiece.

The 4-D and magnifying facility of the plasma balls enabled them to instantly identify duplications or connections between different functions in the Park. As I stood observing I watched as one of the analysts dictated an insertion to a file then tapped the link on the plasma screen twice before spinning to another existing pathway tapping it once to create a new link in the operating system. Instantly this eliminated unnecessary pathways and duplications on the screen as files and strands disappeared in front of me, building an ever more seamless operating system.

As Annie stood watching the Associates, a roar erupted from one side of the room. Instantly the team was congratulated by all the associates with the report that their follow up on a comment expressed on something as simple as the room temperatures in one of the sectors would contribute a 2% reduction in utility costs per annum and a 4% improvement in their environmental targets.

Annie thought carefully of how the Parks 6 functions worked seamlessly together and how the processes and order provided by its structure guided everyone to behave and think in a more organised and methodical manner.

At that she looked up as Desmond from the Sales sector approached her along the raised viewing platform.

"How are you enjoying the tour Annie what do you think of our operations sector?" said Desmond cheerfully.

"Remarkable Desmond...... Desmond I'm wondering if you could answer two questions I have?" asked Annie.

"Of course Annie, how can I help" Desmond said rubbing his hands together enthusiastically.

"I can't quite grasp the whole idea of operations can you explain it to me?"

"Well think of the perfect business as the 'perfect apple pie' you have ever eaten. Now anyone can make an apple pie like anyone can build a business. You need a kitchen, an oven, a cook and all the ingredients for an apple pie. But once you give your customer a taste of that 'perfect apple pie' how do you guarantee every other pie will taste just as good. What if that master cook leaves you or you want to make not 1 but 100 apple pies? How can you guarantee reproducing that perfect apple pie? The secret is the cook book that has every minute detail of how to recreate that 'recipe' or in your case your businesses operating system or manual. The list of ingredients (that secret spice), the weights and measurement of each ingredient (that extra spoon of butter), what order you place the ingredient in the bowl, what temperature you set the oven (is it a gas or electric oven?). At what exact time do you take it out of the oven? Because without that little sheet of paper with that detailed recipe you will never be able reproduce that 'perfect apple pie' ever again, your kitchen, your cook, your larder supplies will be in chaos."

Annie laughed nodding to Desmond.

"Desmond I noticed something today about your associates unlike any other business I have ever visited; the staff never appear *idle, distracted or stressed* why is that?" asked Annie

"Well Annie I have worked in a lot of places before I came to work at the Park. Unlike other businesses the Parks founder recognised that ultimately human beings are a delicate balance of 'emotion and logic' or 'chaos and order'. The chaos is often our emotions what makes us human, unique, quirky individuals something no one can or should change or try to control as this is what makes us unique individuals our personalities. But also as human beings we also crave logic like law and order and rules which often calms our negative emotions. In modern society many people's personal lives are filled with stress, disorder and a lack of focus. Our founder understood that if you were to create a business with a magnificent vision and purpose, a place of order people would queue up to come and work there. The answer to reducing idleness, distraction and stress is achieved through an ethical operating system of clearly defined job descriptions, responsibilities, and principles in your business" said Desmond.

"Thank you Desmond you have really helped, I feel as if I have all the answers I needed now" said Annie.

"Well you know you're always welcome to come back and visit us, we are always here to help." at that Desmond said his goodbyes and sprightly went on his way.'

Annie exited the operations room and slowly began making her way towards the exit of the control centre. Annie felt a new wave of confidence as she skimmed back through her book recapping on the introduction to the 'Black Box ' and what she had learnt from her visit. She reflected on the simple messages of the 'Black Box' and the six roles of Human Resources, Management, Products & Services, Sales, Finance and Operations.

With all the pieces of the jigsaw together she knew her business idea would work, as long as she continued to master the 6 functions of business. She knew that she had just one more unanswered question; to identify two functions in her business that she had greatest strength in, an innovative advantage over her competition. But for now she felt confident enough to move forward with her plans. As she made her way to the tunnel Lauren appeared at the exit.

"So did you find the answers you were looking for?" asked Lauren.

"Yes…..Lauren" Annie said thoughtfully.

"Before you leave I have something for you." said Lauren shaking Annie's hand and presenting her with a pristine white envelope with the 'Designovator's Room' symbol and the hand written words 'Private Invitation'.

"When the time is right you know where we are." said Lauren sincerely.

At that Annie slowly made her way along the tunnel leading out of the Control Centre and into the Parks Gardens. She made her way along the shingle path and simultaneously her sensory jacket slowly increased in temperature adapting to the cool night air as the seams of her clothes transformed her figure into a silhouette of light.

Once more she stood enjoying the peacefulness of the Park, while the magnificence of 'The Library' dominated the Park. The silhouette of its tiny solar leaves glistened like a golden silhouette across the dark indigo skyline while thousands of tiny solar lights randomly scattered across the park lit up the corners of the Park like a field of white daisies and bluebells.

Annie smiled to her self energised by what the evening had revealed. Once more Gran her mentor was right and Annie felt centred and focused finally her mind was clear and she was ready to take on the world.

To be continued…….…...

Part Three: The Designovator's Room

http://www.designovation.co.uk/about

Summary

I Human Resources; leverage of others labour and skills.

I. One must discover and find in life ones single "Material Purpose in Life".

II. Develop a group of "associates" from different disciplines, interests and expertise.

III. Promote the Continual Development of Skills.

IV. Essential Skills: a work ethic, self motivation and common sense.

V. The will to give more than we receive.

VI. The Art of communication.

II Management; The Creation of a definite plan & purpose.

I. Motivating personality.

II. Individual Responsibility& Ethics.

III. Decisive.

IV. Supportive & encouraging.

III Products & Services; serving others with specialised knowledge or skills.

I. Discover what you can create or provide service for to serve humanity.

II. Our care as custodians will be reflected in future generations.

III. Great success comes from specialised skill or knowledge.

IV. Small enterprise is the single most effective source in receiving rewards for your labour and effort.

V. An Inspiring idea or purpose can be found in both humanities hopes and fear.

VI. Find inspiration in seeking to provide solutions.

VII. Focus on areas of Growth.

IV Sales; persistence and the understanding of human desires and fears.

I. Desires.

II. Fears.

III. Art of Persuasion.

IV. Persistence.

V Finances; material wealth through the mastery of financial education.

I. Become a master of finances and economics.

II. The brain is the single essential tool in financial mastery.

III. Master financial education and money will become your servant.

IV. Learn to discern between needs and wants.

V. Learn to discern between assets and liabilities.

VI. Be your own book keeper.

VII. Build your Financial Portfolio in your area of Expertise.

VIII. Financial Timing.

VI. Operations; the power and orchestration of organised systems, processes & people.

I. Develop an Organised Mind.

II. Time the new gold.

III. Invest your time don't spend it.

IV. Work once and get paid forever.

V. Measure everything.

VI. The Price to Pay.

Notes

Introduction

"Before you can field a great team, you have to build a great organisation and all the elements have to be assembled properly."

P61 Leading by Sir Alex Ferguson with Michael Moritz

Chapter 2

P14 Foot notes

Great Universal Stores was founded in 1900 in Manchester, originally called universal stores. In 1930 the company changed its name to Great Universal Stores Limited and in 1931 it was first listed on the London Stock Exchange, at this point it was the leading mail order business in the UK. During the 1930s a second catalogue named "John England" was also produced. In 1937 GUS acquired Kays Catalogue and established mail order Company which had operated from Worcester since the 1880s. Kays stayed as a separate company until the 1980s. In 2004, the company sold its traditional catalogues division to the Barclay twins who merged it into their Littlewoods Empire. This included the iconic Great Universal Stores catalogue, from which the company took its name, and completed the departure of GUS from its original business areas. Around the same time, the Barclays announced the closure of the Littlewoods Index retail chain, the principal rival to Argos in the UK, selling around 35 stores to Argos. In October 2006, GUS plc was demerged into two businesses, Experian and Home Retail Group. Trading in shares of the two groups on the London Stock Exchange began on 11 October, 2006. Home Retail Group is the UK's leading home and general merchandise retailer with sales of over £5.5 billion in 2006. It sells products under two distinctive and complementary retail brands, Argos and Homebase.

Chapter 5

P21 "I am reminded, O King and take this lesson to heart, that there is a wheel on which the affairs of men revolve, and its mechanism is such that it prevents any man from being always fortunate"…….. "This same wheel that prevents any man from being always fortunate may provide also that no one shall be always unfortunate, provided he will take possession of his own mind and direct it to the attainment of some Definite Major Purpose in Life." Croesus, adviser to Cyrus, King of the Persians. Napoleon Hill. "Your Magic Power to be Rich" The Master Key, P325.Penguin

Chapter 6

"There is but one mode by which man can possess in perpetuity all the happiness which his nature is capable of enjoying- that is by the union and co-operation of all for the benefit of each." Source unknown Robert Owen Welsh social reformer and one of the founders of the co-operative movement.

Chapter 8

P36 "I realise that the system within a football club doesn't have the complexity of what is required to design a nuclear submarine, build 50 million mobile phones or organise clinical trials for a new drug. But like every organisation we needed to be well run and had to be sure that our system was deeply ingrained. Our product just happened to be a football team, rather than a car or washing machine, and our whole reason for being was to make sure all the pieces of our product- all the different players- fitted together"P61 'Leading' by Sir Alex Ferguson with Michael Moritz Hodder 2015.

P37 "Youngsters can inject a fantastic spirit in an organisation and a youngster never forgets the person or organisation that gave him his first big chance. He will repay it with a loyalty that lasts a lifetime. For young players nothing is impossible and they will try and run through a barbed-wire fence, while older players will try to find the gate'

P78 'Leading' by Sir Alex Ferguson with Michael Moritz Hodder 2015.

Chapter 10

P44 "…give more responsibility for making decisions to the people who are actually on the firing line, those who deal with the customer's everyday. Good management is going to start listening to the ideas of these line soldiers. Pooling these ideas and disseminating them around their organisations so people can act on them."

Sam Walton 'Made in America" P324 Bantam Books 1992

P45 "My vision, my hope is simply this; that many business leaders will come to see a primary role of business as incubators of the human spirit, rather than factories for the production of more material goods & services." Dame Anita Roddick. "Business as Usual".P25

Chapter 12

P50 "…a lot of folks ask me two related questions all the time. The first one is could a Wal-Mart type story still occur in this day and age? My answer is of course it could happen again. Somewhere out there right now there's someone-probably hundreds of thousands of some ones-with good enough ideas to go all the way. It will be done again, over and over, *providing that someone wants it badly enough to do what it takes to get there. It's all a matter of attitude and the capacity to constantly study and question the management of the business."*

P51 "…. The second question is if I were a young man or woman starting out today with the same sorts of talents and energies and aspirations that I had fifty years ago, what would I do? That answer to that is a little harder to figure out, I don't know exactly what I would do today, but I feel pretty sure *I would be selling something*………." Sam Walton 'Made in America" P326 Bantam Books 1992.

Chapter 13

P57

An asset is a purchase which will increase your wealth & add to your financial income every calendar month.

A liability is a purchase which will reduce your wealth & add to your financial expenses every calendar month.

Robert Kiosaki. "Rich Dad Poor Dad".

Chapter 14

P61 "No society can surely be flourishing and happy of which the far greater part of the members are poor and miserable" Adam Smith Unknown source (The Wealth of Nations)

P63 "In 2013 by year 3 only 6 out of every 10 businesses survived now we have 10 out of every 10. At year 5 instead of only 4 of the 10 original businesses only surviving we have 9. In 2065 instead of only <u>1 business surviving at year 10</u> we have 8 of every original 10 business start-ups not only surviving but also employing 5 or more associates." Adapted for purposes of storyline original statistics from UK Department of Business, Innovation & Skills 2014.

Chapter 16

P70 'working on the business not in the business' Michael E. Gerber "The E-myth Revisited" 1995 Harper Business.

Bibliography

Napoleon Hill. "Your Magic Power to be Rich" The Master Key, P325.

Penguin.

Robert Kiosaki. "Rich Dad Poor Dad".

Michael.E.Gerber. "E-Myth Revisited"

Sir Alex Ferguson. "Leading".

Sam Walton. "Made in America".

Dame Anita Roddick. "Business as Usual".

Napoleon Hill. "Your Magic Power to be Rich"

About the Author

D.F. McKeever is a Scottish Author & Illustrator. She lives in Scotland with her husband and three children. Her passion and interest in personal development & studying successful individuals began in her early teens, while pursuing a career and degree in Design. In addition to working in the family business (manufacturing & engineering company) from her early teens she built her own retail & design business, which she operated for 18 years servicing the public & private sector in Scotland.

The inspiration for "Black Box & White Ball Thinking" came from her experiences in attempting to help her husband get an invention to market the "Shoogle". Her dealings with various Enterprise institutions raised fundamental questions to the lack of understanding of what motivates & makes an Entrepreneur. And what is being taught about the operating models we need for enterprise to succeed in the 21st Century and how creativity & innovation are central to its success.

Gratitude List

Mary & Duncan Burns,
Ronnie & my three children
Margaret & Denis,
Eileen, Theresa, Pauline, Margaret, Michelle, Joanne,
John Paul & Mark
John, James, Joe, Debbie & Leslie
Philip & Paula, John & Cathie McKeever
Annie McKay, Sister Magdalin,
May & Tom, Frances & John, Karen & Allan,
Thomas & Pat, John & Barbara, Rose & Tom, Agnes & Benny,
Jean, Margaret & Denis Hogg
Anna & John, Kathleen & Jim, Jane & Peter, John & Margaret
Sister Martina, Kathleen Brown, Shirley, Sara, Louise, Jackie
Evelyn & John, Mrs Grattan,
Mary & Jim Gibb, Mrs Divers, Mrs Pearson, Father Glakin
Mr Keenan, Mr Quinn, Mrs Miller
Linda Shearer, Dorothy Hogg, Graham Leak, Paul Clifford
Maureen McConnachie, Catriona McLaughlan, Gordon Smith,
Janet McLane, Elaine Symington
Teresa Ward, Nareen Owens, Morag McDowall, Margaret
Scanlin, Theresa O'Neill,
Lorraine McLean, Walter Gregg,
Lauretta McLeod, Elaine Symington, Pat & Jim McGinn,
Des & Anne McLaughlin, John & Mary Kelly, Allana, Mary,
Grant Donnelly.
PSYBT Bill McGilliard, Gail Dunlop, Ken Christopherson,
Jean & John Roonie.

Thank you to Norman Trotter OBE & Gilbert Peddie whom on one memorable afternoon allowed me to share my vision and without personal gain, gave me their time and encouragement when I really needed someone to listen. Thank you for reminding me that one word of encouragement can have a far reaching influence.

Are you an aspiring Entrepreneur?

Sign-up and receive your FREE Business Start-up Handbook <u>NOW!</u>

Just visit us at: http://www.designovation.co.uk

https://youtu.be/uwp7A3U_5hs

https://twitter.com/dfmckeever

www.ingramcontent.com/pod-product-compliance
Lightning Source LLC
Chambersburg PA
CBHW021422210526
45463CB00001B/494